Little Steps

Surviving Anor
Ner

D1439484

By Katharine Wealthall

Published by
Chipmunkapublishing
PO Box 6872
Brentwood
Essex CM13 1ZT
United Kingdom

First published 2005

Copyright © 2005 Katharine Wealthall

A record of this book is in the British Library.

ISBN 1-904697-66-6

http://www.chipmunkapublishing.com

Acknowledgements

In reaching life in recovery and in the writing of this book, I have depended on the love, support and generosity of truly exceptional people.

Thank you so much:

To all the staff at Atkinson Morley's Hospital (1999) without whom I would never have reached life in recovery.

To all the wonderful people who contributed their experiences to this book. Your honesty and bravery has been truly inspirational. I am privileged to know you all.

To Mr. Chris Prestwood and the Eating Disorders Association for their contributions to this book, and also for all their work in helping those with Eating Disorders.

To Jason Pegler, Chipmunkapublishing and Mick Ford (West Norfolk Mind) for seeing the worth in this book and for all their work in the area of mental health.

My immeasurable love and gratitude:

To my incomparable family (including the four legged members) for their unfailing love and support.

To my fabulous, perfect, husband Steve for being my best friend and always believing.

To Andy for always being there and never judging, for being you.

To Patrick for your friendship and for making my going away for treatment possible; your care of Trixie and Sasha helped more than you can know.

Contents

Foreword

I considered it a privilege to be asked to read this very informative, powerful and erudite journey from anorexia nervosa to the point of almost suicide and through, as Katharine put it, to recovery. There are too many issues that this book raises that I can refer to in a forward. Nonetheless, there are a whole host of lessons to be learnt by those people who consider themselves to be the professionals, not the least as it was put by Katharine when given a questionnaire by a psychologist and that is, 'do they not realise that anorexics lie?' Very soberingly, of course, she makes the point that 1 in 20 people who suffer with anorexia nervosa will die as a result of their illness and without appropriate treatment.

As far as hospitalisation is concerned, the reflection on her time in hospital when she was watching 'One Flew Over the Cuckoo's Nest' and others watching stood up to get their medication, is pretty bizarre even by today's standards. Very little seems to have changed since the years when I worked in a psychiatric hospital.

One only has to read the case histories of people like Lorna, Jo, Steve, Kate etc to understand just how difficult this disorder is. Having said that, it is astonishing that almost without exception there is criticism of the present mental health services, for example, delays in treatment i.e. treatment not until one is 24, 34 or even 44 when in fact the illness itself manifests around the fairly early age of 12 – 16. Steve highlights the isolation of a male sharing what he called a female illness.

The overwhelming message is one of hope. Hope that people will start to listen to those service users who know best the problems they face. Hope that self help groups etc will support people particularly at the most dangerous period and that is immediately after treatment, but above all one of hope within each individual. Each of the case histories indicate that there is a hope and a trust in recovery and it is to be hoped that once in recovery 'losing weight no longer becomes a way to disappear.'

**Mick Ford – Chief Executive West Norfolk Mind
February 2005**

Preface

Why Write ...

'Homesickness may feel terrible now, but if you go home with the illness - you will never truly be home'.

These were some of the most valuable words ever spoken to me; it is hard to believe the difference one sentence made. I was in my second month of a 10 month hospital treatment programme for Anorexia and had announced to one of the nurses that I had to go home, couldn't bear to be away any longer. The nurse (one of the many people to which I owe my life 'in recovery') convinced me to stay in treatment with just those few words. Although I have thanked him since, I doubt he can ever know the impact he made.

Anorexia and Bulimia Nervosa rob sufferers of themselves; the real person becomes masked by the intensity of an illness that is both terrifying to suffer from and to witness. During the early stages of my admission, I vowed that once I was in recovery I would have nothing more to do with the illness. I thought it admirable that sufferers who had reached recovery wrote books, set up counselling groups and spent huge amounts of time and energy on helping others, but I felt that I had to leave it behind me - forever.

To a certain extent the naïve belief that I would recover in a way that was complete and forever fuelled this opinion. I wanted to somehow erase the illness and all the pain that had been caused through it (both to myself and those who are close to me). This was when I had little, or no, real understanding of the illness. Through the course of my therapy, however, I became aware that I had been ill all my life (well before the obvious physical symptoms), so how did I expect to blank 25 years?

Also, as I progressed through the treatment programme and towards life in recovery I realised that the illness is a very real part of me, and blanking it would be impossible. As I began to accept this, I felt the desperate need for something good to come out of my horror, out of all the years I had battled to survive.

I also felt increasingly angry at the way the media portray eating disorders and felt the almost overwhelming need to express the reality of the illness, I needed people to understand. One of my worst fears is being seen as someone who chose to be ill; someone who is vain and selfish and just wants to look like a super model, someone who through choice very nearly destroyed her life and the lives of those around her. I cannot bear the possibility that there is anyone who believes that I wanted to be this way. I get so angry when I hear those who are ignorant talking about eating disorders, although I know that it is just that, ignorance, I so want them to understand.

I also felt the need to try and alert people to the difficulties regarding real treatment for eating disorders, and the difficulty in being admitted to one of the few centres that do help sufferers of the illness successfully. I was lucky in that I received excellent treatment, but it was after over a year of 'help' during which I actually deteriorated greatly. It is so important that people know what sort of treatment is needed. Also, although I will be the first to admit that the treatment I finally received was excellent, it had to be hundreds of miles from home (funding wasn't provided for the centre 40 miles from home!), I think this fact was most detrimental to the early stages of my treatment.

Furthermore, as I began to experience life in recovery I was deeply concerned by the lack of information about what it was like to manage the illness, I needed to know that the difficulties I was experiencing was not a relapse but simply survival. A friend of mine I met during treatment put it most accurately when she said 'all books stopped exactly where I needed them to begin', life in recovery is an extremely individual experience but each individual needs to know that the ongoing battle is the reality of life in recovery.

For these reasons, I decided I needed to write a book, this book. It was essential for me that the book emphasise that whilst life in recovery is very difficult, it is possible and also the book needed to be positive and full of hope for life managing the illness instead of being controlled by it.

It is also my intention to create a greater understanding of the nature of the illness and to dispel the myths that surround it by discussing those myths and why their existence is so damaging.

I concluded that my experience alone would not be sufficient to convince anyone of this, or that there truly is light at the end of the tunnel (other than that of the oncoming train!) and so I enlisted the help of the extraordinary people who feature in the coming chapters. Some I met through my time in hospital, others are friends who I met through 'real' life and in time found they were ill too. They are at a variety of stages, some are well into life in recovery, others are slowly moving forwards, others are still within the grip of the illness - all are surviving. All have hope.

I asked them to tell me about how the illness affected their lives, what kind of treatment they received (both positive and negative) and their hopes, and fears for the future. Their frankness and honesty has been a humbling experience and I owe them an enormous amount of thanks, they have my deepest admiration. When I first decided on the style I hoped the book would be, I knew I would be relying on the willingness of others to be involved - the response was overwhelming. All I spoke to felt that a book like this was needed, a book that focused on reaching a real life in recovery, of there being life beyond the grip of the illness. It also needed to be a book that didn't give unnecessary graphic detail of how sufferers abuse themselves, but one that illustrated hope. Hope for sufferers and hope for those who are close to them.

It was also felt by myself and others I spoke to that those who have to witness someone they care about suffering from the illness needed a book containing information that they could empathise with as much as the suffers themselves. When you have been through the illness, it is easy to think that you know what effect your illness (and the consequent behaviour) had on those close to you but no one can possibly truly know how another feels. Therefore, in addition to the personal stories of sufferers I have included accounts of those who have had to witness the pain and suffering, parents and friends who have been frustrated by the feeling of being so powerless, so helpless. I sincerely hope that those who are reading this from that point of view will find some hope and comfort in the knowledge that others have been through similar experience, perhaps more so from the fact that others have watched the sufferer reach life in recovery.

Owing partly to my original motivation to write this book, I felt it important to include information regarding treatment provision, the treatment that sufferers have been offered   (both positive and negative) and the treatment that is needed to reach life in recovery - the treatment that can really help. Many books on eating disorders do not mention treatment that can really help people, preferring to focus on the, sometimes barbaric, often ridiculous treatments that do not help at all.

Additionally, I felt it important to include the thoughts of a professional working to help sufferers; his view of the illness and what is needed to work through the depths of it and live a real life is invaluable, I believe, in showing reaching recovery from all points of view.

One thing I have learnt is that whilst a few people do succeed in fighting the depths of the illness alone, it is a near impossible feat to reach life in recovery without real help. I considered myself 'cured' in 1997, indeed I got myself so physically well that I ran the London Marathon, but as soon as a personal trauma occurred - I experienced a total relapse. I hadn't worked through any of the deep rooted issues that gave my illness its strength and so those issues were all still there. Neither had I accepted the reality of the illness until that point, I knew then that I needed professional help and those professionals saved my life. It would be inappropriate to write this book without the involvement of such a professional. In my opinion treating sufferers of eating disorders must be among the hardest jobs the medical profession has to offer.

The overall intention of the book is to provide a thorough look at eating disorders with a very positive outlook. Suffering from an eating disorder is truly terrifying and frequently unbearable; I often believed death would be a blessed relief. Indeed, as a result of either suicide or physical failure, Anorexia has the highest mortality rate of all mental illness.

In spite of this frightening statistic, the fact that must be focused on by those fighting the illness is that people do survive and come out of the depths of the illness and I am proof of this. The media often portrays such a negative, pessimistic view that the fear connected with the illness for sufferers and those close to them is intensified, I hope this book goes some way to showing that such pessimism can only hold back the hope of survival and life in recovery.

An essential point for all who read this to bear in mind is that the illness is cruel, manipulative, at times disgusting, always dangerous and desperately hard to understand. Those who suffer from the illness are not.

In my experience, people with eating disorders are among the most sensitive, compassionate and beautiful people I have ever met. They are also people who are very gifted, very talented and capable of achieving so much. It is extraordinary that the illness is able to mask such a great deal, or at the very least it is able to prevent the sufferers from recognising their positive attributes. I hope that the positivity contained within the following pages will help those who read it to see deeper into who they really are, who they could be beyond the confines of the illness.

I also hope it will help those on the outside to understand the difficulty in fighting the illness, but that they will see the hope in trying. The unknown future of life in recovery is almost as frightening as staying in the illness (sometimes more frightening), particularly for those who have been locked in associated behaviours for many years. Therefore it must be recognised that the sufferer will struggle reaching life in recovery and will continue to struggle during life in recovery, but that does not mean that he/she won't make it and live a very full and real life - the saying 'where there is life, there's hope' has never been more appropriate.

When beginning my own long road into recovery there was one thing I knew I had to find out, I needed to know who I would be beyond the grip of the illness - what the future would hold for me if I were in control of the illness and was well. I hope that this book may help convince others that it is worth finding out who they are too.

Chapter 1.　　　Myths and Misconceptions

One of the greatest difficulties facing sufferers of eating disorders in acknowledging the illness and receiving treatment, is the widespread lack of knowledge and real understanding. There are many myths surrounding the nature of eating disorders and varied misconceptions regarding the cause of them and the 'type' of person who is likely to suffer from them.

The existence of these myths and misconceptions is extremely damaging. Many people have little or no knowledge regarding the true nature of the illness and therefore are likely to believe whatever they read or can assume. Unfortunately this also applies to a number of the medical profession.

The existence of these myths and misconceptions contributes greatly to the general lack of understanding surrounding the illness. This lack of understanding is a frightening thing for sufferers to face, particularly when it comes from those close to them or from their Doctor. It heightens the feelings of isolation and vulnerability and it can often seem that the mountain to reach recovery is just too great to climb.

The thought of having to do it alone is too terrifying to consider. This can also lead to an intensifying of the symptoms as it increases beliefs such as 'this is all my fault', 'I deserve to feel like this' and 'there's no way out'. Similar to people suffering from depression, sufferers of eating disorders are often told to 'snap out of it' or 'pull yourself together'. It would seem that it is often easier to dismiss the problem than it is to try and understand what is really going on. It is essential that the myths and misconceptions are dispelled to ensure this situation improves.

'Slimmer's Disease'...

All of the people who contributed to this book (and other sufferers I have spoken to) have experienced the criteria for diagnosis being solely relating to their body weight, and treatment focussing on simply increasing their body weight. This in itself shows a distinct lack of understanding regarding the true nature of the illness. The idea that an eating disorder is simply about physical image and is therefore just a diet that went too far is as ignorant as it is dangerous.

To classify it as 'slimmer's disease' (as was and often still is the case) denies the sufferer the chance of true recovery and any hope of a real future. Whilst the weight and consequent appearance of sufferers (particularly anorexics) is clearly the most obvious of the symptoms it is simply that – a symptom. This is purely an external expression of inner pain, a desperate symbol of the intensity of the feelings buried within.

It is important to note at this point that often anorexics and bulimics are very seriously ill whilst maintaining an acceptable, even normal, body weight. The preoccupation with food, weight and body image are quite simply the tip of a deadly destructive iceberg. The drive for thinness, so often thought to be the most major indication of eating disorders, is not always present – the complicated, destructive thought processes always are.

Similarly, it is grossly inaccurate to assume that those who are losing weight through the effects of an eating disorder are vain and have a fear of weight gain solely due to an aesthetic dislike for bodies carrying excess (or even normal) weight. Whilst it is true that amongst many sufferers there is a fear of gaining weight, this fear is simply the focus the illness is using as avoidance for facing all other issues, or indeed ordinary life situations.   Sufferers will state that they can't bear to gain weight but this is simply the illness causing them to believe that they must be thin, gaining weight would be a failure and another failure would be too much. Also removing the focus of restricting food makes them vulnerable to all sorts of feelings that are too frightening to cope with.

A Matter of Choice…

Through ignorance regarding the illness, it is often implied that it is the person's choice to be ill and if only they changed their attitude then everything would be fine! One of the most essential things that people need to understand about eating disorders is that, (as with all mental illness) the sufferer does not choose to be ill. It may be true that they are initially aware of the decision to starve, binge etc but that decision is being enforced through other factors and is not a conscious decision in the usual accepted sense.

It is also important to note that on the surface, sufferers often have a great deal to be positive about – for example, great talent, wonderful family, comfortable life style etc. The fact that this is often the case is further evidence that no one would ever choose to behave in a way that would risk losing it all. Indeed these positive things can lead to an intensifying of negative thinking such as, 'I am so lucky, I am terrible for not appreciating it all' or, 'why do other people suffer much worse than me but don't become ill – it must be my fault'.

Existing within the illness is a terrifying horror, it makes little sense and yet the sufferer feels trapped by thoughts, feelings and associated behaviours – regardless of how damaging and dangerous they are. I can confidently state that no sufferer of an eating disorder would choose to be that way.

Taking Control …

It is often assumed that eating disorders are to do with taking control, other aspects of life cannot be controlled but intake of food (for example) can. People often find themselves in a situation/environment that was chosen for them or forced upon them; the result is one of feeling trapped.

Being expected to do well at school, followed by going to university (for example) can be seen as great pressure for anyone. To a person with an eating disorder, however, that pressure is believed to be an overwhelming responsibility and, indeed, necessity. Failure would not be just failure for the individual at the time, it would be seen as a failure for all time, another reason to feel hate for oneself and to believe that one is an enormous disappointment to all around them.

When the mind reacts to common difficulties (experienced by many) in such an extreme way, a way that is well beyond normal stress/disappointment, it is little wonder that many find a degree of solace in controlling some aspect of their lives. In such a situation, however, the focus of control must be something that can be kept secret – something private. This could be for any number of reasons, the most likely being that it is believed that the control may be taken away by anyone who knew, or that they feel ashamed of what is happening and do not want to be the cause of further disappointment.

It is important to note that the need for control is not the main driving force behind the illness in all sufferers, however, and must never be generalised as such. Furthermore, it is very important to recognise that whilst, for many sufferers, the initial overwhelming feeling may be about a need for control, the illness is very strong and the control is very quickly taken from the conscious, rational thoughts of the sufferer.

Selfishness...

I once had the misfortune to read a magazine article that was written by a (allegedly) recovered anorexic. This piece was making the claim that people with eating disorders (anorexics in particular) are selfish and are ill by their own doing. It also stated that these people often behave in such a way simply to hurt those who care about them.

I found it shocking and angered me deeply that such an article should receive publication space. Obviously the magazine printed it because it was a different angle and therefore likely to be controversial. Whilst it must be acknowledged that every experience of the illness is different and this lady is clearly entitled to her opinion, such generalisations are very damaging and dangerous.

All the people suffering from the illness that I have met could certainly never be described as selfish, indeed more often than not their main aim in life is to do as much for others as possible. They want nothing more than to please others and be seen as positively by others as possible. Hardly the behaviour of someone who is selfish!

Whilst it is true to say that many behaviours associated with eating disorders could be construed as self obsessed (e.g. constant studying of body shape) these give no true pleasure or long-term satisfaction and indeed only serve to give further fuel to the negative mindset. Doing things for others, however, gives some relief and allows at least a degree of enjoyment (albeit very brief).

From my own experience, the fact that I have caused my family hurt was (and still is) one of my greatest regrets throughout all my years with the illness. To cause pain and immense worry to those who love you must be one of the greatest injustices anyone can commit, I have caused so much pain and if I could change that there is no doubt that I would. I know that other sufferers feel the same.

Attention Seeking ...

There is also the common misconception that the illness is simply people craving attention. When I was at school and started showing the physical signs of the illness (aged 14) I was the target for bullying from a group of girls who decided that I was an attention seeker – they spread their opinion around, even writing it all over their pencil cases and books. Everywhere I went at school I had people shouting taunts at me etc, surely if I craved attention then I would have succeeded in my aim and would have stopped!

Such focussed attention had a hugely negative effect on my psychological state, I firmly believe this accelerated the onset of more severe associated behaviours and deepened the beliefs of my negative mindset. Whilst it could well be the case that many people who develop eating disorders are in a situation where their needs are ignored, and this could well be a trigger for negative thoughts and feelings, it is not the 'purpose' of the illness.

Even to someone who has little understanding of the illness surely it would seem ridiculous to believe that something so terrifying and dangerous would have such a basic aim. In any case, this is further implying that the illness is a matter of choice and can be turned on and off at will. Similar to the need for control, the sufferer may start out thinking very rationally, for example, 'if I lose weight then they'll notice me'. This very rapidly becomes insignificant to the strength and controlling irrational influence of the illness, the negative mindset (see below for further detail).

For many with eating disorders, having people giving them a lot of attention is terrifying and it is the last thing they want. Such attention can also lead to intensifying the feelings of guilt often carried by the sufferer by their feeling and belief that they do not deserve it and hate to cause inconvenience and worry. A common fear shared by many sufferers of eating disorders is one of social situations i.e. a considerable number of people. Many become virtually reclusive whilst in the depth of the illness and find it almost impossible to relate to other people. I found it almost impossible to go out without a member of my immediate family, it was as though I was clinging to those I felt understood me (at least understood me to a certain extent) attention was the very last thing I wanted.

It is a strange yet interesting fact however that this intense fear of attention became really prominent when people knew that I was ill, when I had reached the stage of being desperate for recovery.

Influence of the Media ...

The above facts are important when considering the portrayal of eating disorders in the media. On average, not a week goes by without the tabloid press 'exposing' some celebrity or other as suffering from either anorexia or bulimia.

There is rarely any mention of the possibility that they have simply made a concerted effort to lose weight in order to be able to wear the latest fashions or to look 'acceptable' at an awards ceremony (for example). In general, society likes its idols to be physically attractive, and for the majority of cultures attractive means slim. After all, we do not have assessments of celebrity's personalities on our walls; we do not have monthly detail of stars favourite things on a calendar. We have pictures of their faces and often their whole body; which is generally slim often thin.

It is most likely the case that the majority of celebrities claimed by the media to be suffering are just fulfilling the role carved out for them by general opinion within society. They often have to follow very strict diet regimes to achieve the required shape, and frequently they end up looking too thin and gaunt. However, being on a diet, even one that takes a person to a low weight, does not necessarily mean an eating disorder and it must not be assumed that it does.

It is a depressing truth that the same publications who are quick to make these assumptions are also even quicker to highlight if a star has gained weight – indeed they positively revel in a holiday shot of a celebrity wearing very little and showing a less than perfectly toned body (whether male or female).

Obviously, noticeable weight loss is cause for concern, especially in a person that had no excess to lose. However, the reasons for it need to be established before assumptions and consequent (often inaccurate) conclusions are drawn.

It is also often considered that pictures of thin celebrities can cause people to 'become' anorexic. This is absolute nonsense. It is impossible to 'catch' an eating disorder, by looking at pictures or any other way. It is true to say that such images can reinforce feelings of inadequacy in a person predisposed to have an eating disorder (or indeed in any healthy person) but this will only be adding to feelings that are already there through the negative mindset.

It really cannot be emphasised enough that eating disorders are to do with emotional and psychological thoughts, feelings and consequent actions. Weight loss (and indeed gain) can be a symptom but alone is not conclusive evidence of the illness.

A Type ...

A further misconception is that there is a very specific type of person who is more likely to suffer from an eating disorder. Generally it has been suggested that the 'typical' sufferer will be female, middle class, adolescent, intelligent, academic high achiever and perfectionist.

Care must be taken with this definition (as with all stereotypes) however, as there are sufferers who do not fit the bill. Clearly these attributes are true of many (otherwise the belief would never have come about!) but in my experience, sufferers come from all backgrounds, all classes and are not all significantly high achievers academically.

As with most things involving human beings it is extremely difficult to conclude a definitive type and attempting to do so can run into complications regarding accurate diagnosis and treatment. For example if a person did not fit the definitive mould then it may be the case that the problem is unrecognised by medical professionals for longer. This again relates to the major problem of allowing generalisations to occur.

Every single person and experience of the illness is different and this must be acknowledged in order for diagnosis to be accurate and treatment to be successful.

Victims of Abuse...

Yet another widely believed myth is that the majority of people with eating disorders have experienced some form of abuse as a child, often sexual abuse.

This is a dangerous assumption to believe as it can lead to false conclusions being drawn about the individual and consequently, their families. Such thinking can also prevent (or delay) the genuine areas of difficulty being identified and helped.

A parent who has contributed to this book (see chapter 3) states that one of the counsellors her daughter saw spent weeks of weekly sessions trying to establish how much her parents had abused her as a child – without even questioning whether she'd been abused at all! This parent believes that this wasted a huge amount of time and was totally unproductive. I would guess that such an approach would put a patient off seeing any professional. It may even intensify the illness through feelings of guilt that their family was being thought of in such a way. Or, they may even feel that they are wasting the time of the counsellor because they are not able to speak about what they are being asked (because it didn't happen, not because it is emotionally hard).

This would, of course, apply to any assumption made by any professional, not just regarding abuse. Again it is important to note here that people with eating disorders often feel acutely and solely responsible for all that goes on around them – even when it is the action of someone else or something they simply can't control.

When considering concerns regarding assumptions made by counsellors' et al, this is not to say that abuse never features in the background of someone who has developed an eating disorder, it very frequently does. Any form of abuse can be a very definite trigger for the manifestation of the illness. This is mainly because abuse leads to feelings such as self-loathing, disgust, fear and intense humiliation (amongst others). Indeed, it can be noted that the thoughts and feelings that can be identified within victims of abuse are very, very similar to those experienced by anyone suffering from an eating disorder (a victim of abuse or not).

It must not be construed, however that all people who develop an eating disorder have suffered abuse simply because the emotional/psychological state is very similar. Of course, counsellors, therapists etc must always consider the possibility of some form of abuse because so many cases are apparent within eating disorders. However, they must surely take care that they do not make assumptions (of this or any other kind) as this may jeopardise the patient's treatment and consequent progress.

The awareness of how easy and how damaging it can be to make assumptions should also be something that friends and relatives of sufferers consider in order that they are as helpful as possible. Avoiding assumptions and generalisations also goes a great distance towards treating the person as the individual they are, rather than putting them into a neat box labelled through their diagnosis.

Where eating disorders are concerned (as with so many illnesses) the sooner the patient receives the right treatment the better (see chapter 6) and therefore it is important not to spend valuable time on areas that are not there when there are likely to be many areas that need time spent on working them through.

Men and Eating Disorders …

A further misconception often believed is that eating disorders is a condition that only affects women. Whilst it is true that around 90% of people developing an eating disorder are female, that leaves 10% that are male. It is also interesting to note that amongst children who develop eating disorders (this is happening in increasing numbers, some as young as 8) up to 25% are boys (figures taken from Eating Disorders Association information).

This misconception that eating disorders are a 'woman's thing' could be based in the belief that the illness is about weight, shape and vanity. Surely as it is women that pore over beauty magazines and want to look like models it is only them that will get the illness! This, of course, is a stereotypical generalisation of any woman, not just of those with an eating disorder, and also ignores the fact that men are becoming increasingly concerned with their appearance and many have cosmetic products and magazines just as women do!

It is important to note again here that the illness is about thoughts, feelings and consequent behaviours – thousands of people (both male and female) take an interest in their appearance but don't develop the illness.

To believe that eating disorders only affect females implies that the negative mindset and the thoughts and feelings that go with it are exclusively female. This is clearly not the case; the thoughts and feelings are human traits neither exclusively female nor male but can be experienced by anyone.

It may be argued then that the illness should affect females and males in equal numbers, there is, after all a huge discrepancy between 90% and 10%. Whilst this is clearly true, there is the possibility that many men are suffering from some form of the illness – they are simply not being diagnosed.

The myth that it is a female illness consequently makes it quite a stigma for a man to admit that he is experiencing such problems. A male contributor to this book (see chapter 3) clearly states that he believes his illness has not been taken seriously, nor has he received the correct treatment, mainly because he is male.

Although male cases of eating disorders that are diagnosed often appear to be clinically similar, if not indistinguishable from the illness in females (Margo 1987; Schneider and Agras 1987), there is the possibility (put to me by Mr. Chris Prestwood, see chapter 5) that many men suffer from the same thought processes etc that form the basis to eating disorders and yet those thoughts and feelings result in different behaviours.

For example, obsessive exercise/bodybuilding or regular drinking binges could be symptoms of a very similar mental state. Such behaviours could well be providing a desperately needed focus and consequently masking genuine thoughts and feelings that may well be serious insecurities. Spending excessive hours in a gym, for example, may be an effort to achieve what they may perceive to be physical perfection i.e. 'if I look better, I'll be better' or perhaps it may be an attempt at the type of control described earlier.

If this is the case, it could then be concluded that, whilst the illness does appear to be predominantly female, that does not mean that men cannot be sufferers – more that the symptoms may be different.

Eating disorders are not a diet that went too far, they are not the product of vanity or the need to look like a supermodel or a film star. They are not a matter of choice, nor are they an elaborate ploy to get attention.

Eating disorders are a complicated, terrifying, deadly illness and whilst they are baffling, the need to understand should not be fulfilled by simplifying them as 'slimmer's disease' or any other term that so belittles the overwhelming horror that is this all consuming illness.

Eating disorders destroy lives in so many ways it is vital that understanding be increased, even if only to dispel the myths and misconceptions.

Understanding the Anorexic Mind ...

Each individual case of an eating disorder is very complex and extremely difficult to understand (for those suffering as well as those observing). In order to achieve any level of understanding, it is essential to recognise that the mind of a person with an eating disorder works differently to a healthy mind.

Perhaps the easiest way of understanding this is to think in terms of everyone having a mindset, that is, the way in which one thinks and consequently behaves/deals with life. It can be considered that there are positive and negative mindsets. I first heard of this concept through the work of Peggy Claude-Pierre (The Secret Language of Eating Disorders – Transworld Publishers) and it made a lot of sense to me. This is not to say, however, that this is an explanation of how the mind can work that everyone would agree with but I believe it helpful for those who are completely baffled by this complex illness.

The positive and negative mindsets are not mutually exclusive of course – human beings in general have a mixture of positive and negative thinking. Sufferers of eating disorders, however, could certainly be considered to have an exceptionally strong negative mindset which not only creates difficulties dealing with life and all it holds, but also determines the person to think in a way that is damaging and destructive to themselves. In many cases, the sufferer is aware of what is going on but they are simply powerless to halt the progression of the illness.

During my most serious bout of anorexia (in its obvious physical form) I could see what was happening and I wanted it over before it began and yet it was like looking at someone else, I was utterly powerless to halt the destruction. It was as though there were two sides to me, the positive rational side and its negative, irrational counterpart (others say the same, see chapter 3). Even now, in recovery, I still experience this conflict.

The medical explanation for this is that the chemicals in the brain become unbalanced as the body tries to cope with the effects of starvation and malnutrition. It is very important to recognise that anyone with an eating disorder will be suffering from malnutrition even if they not obviously underweight. This chemical imbalance prevents the person from thinking clearly and indeed can make functioning at all very, very difficult. It is as though walking around in a fog, nothing is really clear and a person in this state finds everything complicated and even simple tasks seem an impossible challenge.

Although this is an accurate description of what is happening in the brain in medical terms, the bizarre, horrifying changes are evident before the effects of malnutrition have taken hold. As a sufferer I can confidently state that the illness should be understood as being a psychological condition that is exacerbated by the biochemical changes that occur as a result of the behaviours induced by the psychological and emotional disorder.

The mind of someone with an eating disorder becomes closed off to hearing or seeing situations for what they really are. The brain behaves in such a way that only the negative perception of any given circumstance is acknowledged. To put in more simple turns, ask any person with an eating disorder if a glass is half full or half empty – the glass is always half empty!

It is as though the person is not allowed to feel happy or to feel good about themselves; even if they are able to value aspects of their lives these things are masked by the negativity. I have always been so lucky with many aspects of my life but I always experienced enormous guilt about that. The profoundly negative mindset and the consequent illness just did not allow me to feel I was worthy of anything positive.

Whilst this general view of a mindset can be helpful, it is essential to acknowledge that eating disorders are very complex and vary so much from one sufferer to another.

What Causes the Illness?

Whilst I am absolutely convinced that sufferers are born predisposed to developing the illness, what lies at the root of this predisposition is by no means conclusive.

There is much research that suggests that 'a person's genetic make up may make them more likely to develop an eating disorder' (Eating Disorders Association - information leaflet). Studies involving members of the same family suffering from the illness are a very popular subject amongst researchers. Indeed, during my time in hospital there was a girl who had been involved in many research studies, as she, her twin and their mother had suffered from anorexia for many years. Research in Holland found that 11% of anorexia patients studied shared the same genetic mutation. The same study concluded that the chances of developing the condition were 1 in 200 but where a family member had the illness, the chances rise to just 1 in 30. Regarding twins, it was concluded that, when one twin develops the illness, there is a 50% chance that the other twin will also do so (Van Elburg et al 2001). Although all studies have, to date, failed to be 100% definitively conclusive, the genetic theory continues to be very popular.

There are also other areas of research, for example, it has been suggested that a lack of the substance AgRP (Agouti Related Protein), found in the brain, may be linked to anorexia (Adan et al 1994).

A very recent study (Lask et al 2005) has found that reduction in blood flow to certain areas of the brain is associated with the inability to block intrusive thoughts and visuo-spacial ability is compromised. This brain dysfunction is found in about two-thirds of young people with anorexia nervosa and provides more information about the site and nature of the neurobiological contribution. Although further studies have to be conducted in this area it is really encouraging that researchers are looking closely at the brain itself as well as the genetic possibilities.

In addition to possible biological/organic causes it has been considered that the influence of someone in the family could affect thinking through their attitude to food (this theory is misleading however as it implies the illness is about food).

Furthermore, it is often the case that a traumatic event can trigger the onset of anorexia or bulimia nervosa (bereavement, being bullied, upheaval in the family e.g. divorce). However, why some people develop an eating disorder and others in similar situations do not, is still unclear. This lends great weight to the belief that people are born predisposed to developing the condition.

As detailed above, thinking in terms of a negative mindset may help make some sense of the way people with eating disorders behave, but still does not identify the root cause. There are many other aspects of eating disorders that need to be explained or, indeed, brought to attention as often things go unnoticed – masked by the blatantly obvious physical symptoms.

It is essential that research into the root cause of eating disorders

continues although, unfortunately, it will always be of a lower priority to other illnesses. When it is finally established, treatment of the illness will be much more effective as it will be tackling the stem of the illness not just management of the mindset and consequent behaviours.

Identifying Common Traits and Helping the Sufferer...

Whilst there is still no established initial cause for the illness nor any definitive type of person, it is important to acknowledge that there are certain patterns of thinking that are evident within in the majority of sufferers whilst in the illness.

These include; an intense dislike for themselves (developing into the need to hurt/punish themselves), the belief of being a failure – of not being good enough at anything, the feeling that they have nothing to offer and nothing of worth to say and the belief that they are responsible for the well being of those around them and have the power to fix all that is wrong. It is interesting to note that all these thoughts, feelings and beliefs are ones that are constantly demanding far too much of any one person.

The need for perfection, if it is evident, is seen as perfection in absolute terms – nothing less is satisfactory. When aiming for such impossibly high standards it is obvious to objective observers that such perfection is unattainable and yet those in the illness are simply not allowed to rest from striving to achieve it. The negative mindset is such that the sufferer firmly believes that they are undeserving of a real life with any happiness if they cannot achieve the self imposed standards.

Indeed, many sufferers feel the need to hurt themselves as a punishment for not achieving, for not being good enough. Causing oneself hurt can be achieved in any number of ways and will be individual to each sufferer, perhaps one of the least recognised is that many will deny themselves things that could give them happiness/pleasure. For example, I was in hospital with a girl whose parents had brought in a television for her to have in her room – it never came out from its box under her desk as she felt she didn't deserve it.

When attempting to make sense of this aspect of the illness, it is necessary to understand that the sufferer just cannot see that they are a deserving person, that they are worthwhile and special. When in the depths of the illness all they can focus on is what they have done wrong, what they haven't done and the sort of person they want to be. Whilst this could be seen as being as simple as focussing on body weight and shape, i.e. 'if I was thinner I'd be a better person', the real focus is much darker 'I'm evil, I wish I was dead', for example.

This negativity does not mean, however, that those close to a sufferer should not continually challenge these powerful thoughts as such help will pay off (even if it takes a long time). The essential point is for relatives, friends etc to remain patient and simply keep reaffirming what is, in fact, the truth about the person.

When in the grip of the illness but still maintaining the pretence of being 'fine', I was often the centre of attention. I love acting and all through school I was involved in all the drama work I could, this led people to conclude that I had huge self – confidence. This is an assumption made of many people with eating disorders however, having asked other sufferers about this I found that this assumption is most frequently made of bulimics - the physical symptoms often being a lot less obvious and therefore the illness more easily hidden. Such feigned self – confidence is simply part of the elaborate disguise to prevent anyone asking what is wrong.

The secret struggle and the intense pain have to be closely guarded or the person believes they will be unable to cope, unable to be 'normal'. In my own experience after a successful acting performance I'd then feel that I was a fraud and would hate myself even more. The illness was so strong it masked who I was to such an extent that even I couldn't see the real me. To this day such thinking is hard for me to understand, I do know, however that many people with eating disorders are desperate to be liked and to belong. It is true that the majority of people would admit to wanting these things but for someone with an eating disorder it is yet another thing that they measure in impossible levels.

Even when surrounded by people, someone with an eating disorder will feel permanently alone and simply cannot admit that they are liked – they certainly can't accept that people would want to spend time with them. Even if all the evidence is to the contrary, they will find it very hard to believe that they are worth anyone being around. Many will also find it difficult to accept that they are deserving of being loved and will often push those who love them away because they believe they are not worthy of something so special as love.

Even when feeling unworthy of receiving love, the love felt for others is often clung to as though it were the final piece of wreckage from a sinking ship. Without a doubt, it was how much I love my family that kept me fighting. Even though I never felt as though I deserved their love, I wanted to keep fighting to become worthy of that love. I was often so cruel to them though, I truly felt the only way to keep them loving me was to push them away so that they wouldn't know what I believed to be the 'real me' (see chapter 2).

Through the darkest times I was haunted by the terrifying thought that if my parents truly knew what I was like they wouldn't love me anymore. I know that other sufferers have experienced this type of feeling; one girl in hospital had not phoned her Mum for weeks because as she found out more about herself through therapy, she believed her Mum wouldn't want her. This action made her incredibly miserable and was of course based on total fiction and yet she believed it was the only thing to do to keep her Mum's love.

Something that is hard for those close to the sufferer to cope with is the apparent reluctance to receive treatment/accept help. This must not, however, be construed as wanting to be ill. For many sufferers (myself included) they have not experienced a life without the illness (or at least not one they can really remember) and the thought of who they will be and what it will be like without it is often more terrifying than the horror of staying in the illness. This will often result in the sufferer talking in very confusing ways; one minute they are begging for help, the next they are begging to be left alone.

This behaviour is hard to explain yet learning to live without an all consuming psychological condition is rather like being a small child who loses sight of their parent in a busy department store - where to go and what to do is impossible to rationalise when you have never done it before. I have often referred to my own recovery as being like a child trapped in an adult body, people who meet me make the normal assumptions you would of an adult and I have normal adult responsibilities. For me, however, every day is a battle to cope with the way the world works and being a responsible adult in normal ways; for example, not hurting myself if things go wrong, not feeling to blame/responsible if things are difficult for others.

Although I am in recovery and am working to achieve this normality, I can vividly remember the intense fear of what it would be like without the illness, indeed I still experience that fear now I am living it. For a period of my treatment, I felt as though I wasn't anybody without the illness that had defined and controlled me all my life. It takes time to rebuild, to relearn but it can be done and therefore, to further emphasise, a reluctance to leave the illness is not the sufferer wanting to be ill – it is the fear of what is to come and being ready to find out. Sufferers must be constantly reassured that it will be worth finding out who they can be, what their life could be like. Those close to them must keep sight of the real person and do all they can to keep affirming that reality.

The most important thing to remember is that generalisations and stereotypes are potentially very dangerous and extremely damaging to the chances of truly reaching recovery. It is all too easy to draw inaccurate conclusions about the illness; indeed there is a wealth of misinformation to be found through the press and magazines. The illness is individual to each sufferer and varies in degrees of intensity yet it must never be ignored or dismissed as nonsense or vanity.

Chapter 2.   Me.

I am an anorexic. I have anorexia nervosa.

I have had this illness all my life and know that I will have this illness for the rest of my life.

Accepting that has been one of my biggest challenges.

A therapist in hospital told me early on in treatment that I was afraid to own my illness, that I was reluctant to accept that it was a part of me. At the time I was incensed. She had to be wrong, it was quite clearly a 'thing' I just had to get rid of – in order to fight it, and I had to believe that. I now know that she was absolutely right. This illness is a part of me. It dictates to a great extent how my brain operates; how I think, how I feel, what I do – who I am.

Anorexia controlled me for many years, and even though it no longer controls me, it is a daily struggle to keep it that way.   I find it very worrying and it makes me quite angry that at no time through my 8 month treatment programme did anyone even hint at how difficult life in recovery would be.

In writing this book I feel it is essential that the reality of life with this illness is expressed. In order to do so, I realise it is important that I tell my story, the reality of this disorder for me. This is by no means an easy task however as there is so much to tell, and yet so little that makes any real sense, the illness is so complex.

My life has been a combination of events and triggers that have given the illness I was born with the opportunity to develop.

Before Treatment ...

When I was very little my mum says she noticed many different and disturbing aspects of my behavior that, at the time she just put down to individuality. With the benefit of hindsight, however, she knows that these were the early signs that something was very wrong with my thinking, and consequent reactions.

For example, there was a time when a family friend had a premature baby and another friend was sick with Leukemia, at school I was working on the Red Indians and we had to make a little pouch called a bulla which contained a wish and was worn round the neck. My wish was that they would both get better, they both died. Mum remembers my reaction as 'deeply worrying', I was in bed and she came in to talk to me about it all, I just turned and faced the wall and refused to speak. Even though it was so many years ago, I can remember how I felt, I felt guilty and I felt responsible. I thought they had died because I had been greedy asking for two wishes to come true, I genuinely believed that I had something to do with their deaths, indeed I believed it was my fault.

Soon after, whilst we were away on holiday, one of my guinea pigs, Pepper, died. They had been well looked after by a friend and it was just old age but again I believed it was my fault. I remember so clearly walking down the garden carrying Salt (the remaining one) and telling her over and over again that I was sorry, that I hadn't split them up on purpose. Again, the guilt and sense of responsibility I felt were enormous, the sense of loss overwhelming.

These were the first occasions I experienced loss through death and it still remains the major trigger for my illness, in spite of the fact I am now an adult and well able to hear and understand the 'rational' reasoning. A therapist in hospital said I believe I have 'an omnipotent power', the ability to control everything, fix everything, make everything better and she was absolutely correct. Everything is somehow my fault, my responsibility.

When we were little we were well aware that our parents had severe financial problems, I remember sneaking into their room and leaving my money box on their bed, I genuinely believed that I was able to make it right, stop them fighting, make them happy. Increasingly throughout life I have struggled with the notion that if my parents really knew me, they wouldn't love me. As a little girl I was always trying to make things better for them, give them reasons to love me. To this day I believe I should have been able to do more to help. My parents eventual divorce 6 years ago saw confirmation of my failure to make them happy, to make them love each other – was this ever my job? Of course not, but to my mindset, I love them both so much I should have been able to make them happy, to make things right.

In addition to this, I have always been excessively compassionate (this is a common trait of anorexics and indeed other mental health patients), to the point where the negative actions of others deeply upset me in a manner which prays on my mind and eats away at me.

For example, I vividly remember one occasion during lunchtime at primary school, we were sitting out on picnic benches to eat our lunch and several other children and two dinner ladies were killing wasps. I was absolutely horrified and told them to stop, they just laughed at me and I run off down the field to cry about it by myself. I didn't want anyone to see me crying, the art of concealment began very young. During that afternoons lessons I felt totally disconnected from everyone and everything around me, I can still picture myself there, a vision of normality; long blond hair in a pony tail, totally healthy looking but already the inner turmoil was building. I did not fit in with those people that place – this was the first occasion I can remember feeling that way, a feeling that was to increase in frequency and intensity throughout my life.

Excessive compassion is a trait which has stayed with me and still I cannot bear any kind of cruelty, towards anything (I have been a strict vegetarian for over 17 years for example). Whilst the majority of decent, caring people are uncomfortable with watching images of war (for example) on the news, for me it is taken to the absolute extreme. My immediate gut reaction to any form of cruelty (on whatever level) is one of total abhorrence. In so many respects it makes life very difficult but on balance, I like that I am this way, I would rather have excessive compassion and sensitivity than accept what seems to be becoming increasingly commonplace in our society.

As I progressed through my childhood the most common factors of my behaviour were not that dissimilar to many healthy children, except that it was so extreme. I was intensely shy with strangers and really panicked if I had to do anything, go anywhere without my parents or my brother (Nick) or sister (Helen). If people came to visit I would always hang around my Mum or Dad, preferably in a room away from the visitors (if one of them was preparing food in the kitchen for example) – even if they were people I had known all my life. I embarrassed easily and preferred people to not talk to me at all rather than be left with the inevitable feeling that I had done or said something stupid/wrong.

It was so easy to let Nick and Helen take centre stage, Nick was extremely intelligent and very funny, he was instantly popular with adults and other children alike. Helen was cute, pretty, very intelligent and so confident and endearing that even when being naughty she was totally appealing. Not much has altered in those respects to be honest!
In reality I was not that different to them, at home I talked endlessly (to anyone or anything), if there was nothing specific to talk about I would make up stories. I also had very similar intelligence and sense of humour to them but the illness was always dominant, even from that early age, and the consequent insecurities were overwhelming.

As time passed it became more difficult to be myself at all. I do not blame anyone for this and it only began to bother me when incidents started to occur that made me feel that all I was, was an outer shell, nothing more. For example, there was an occasion we had been to watch Helen performing in a children's opera and we were at the after show party. My parents were talking to a couple they knew and Nick and I were introduced to them, the man looked at me and said 'ahh the looks of the family' then started talking to Nick, no one said another word to me. I just stood there and felt so isolated, so lost – it should have been a compliment that made me feel good but I was so insecure that all it did was confirm my belief that I was nothing of worth.

Throughout adolescence, I experienced what are usually thought of as stereotypical factors in the development of an eating disorder, I was bullied at school (apparently my voice was too 'posh' for a Norfolk comprehensive), my parents were constantly unhappy with each other and home was therefore perpetually difficult but for me these were not the main triggers, merely contributory factors to an increasingly deeply disturbed mindset.

Much more significantly, events in my life occurred that became the most major triggers and have remained a driving force for my illness. I did a number of things wrong and the idea developed in my head that I was evil, that I was thoroughly unworthy of having anything good in my life. I believed that I had to be punished for all the things I had done wrong, hadn't managed to do and that I had to earn all the good things that were in my life. This belief was (and often still is) totally real and any rational thoughts were utterly squashed.

The other prominent area of thought was the increasing presence of obsessive thoughts and behaviours; these were always directed at my pets (my rabbit, guinea pig, dog and pony) who were the absolute centre of my world. I devised a fixed routine of looking after them that increased in its specification through my teenage years, everything had to be absolutely right for them and that included how much time I spent with them. For example, throughout the last years of school I would be up at 5.00 a.m. every day to ensure that I spent enough time with each of them before going to school.

During those years Whisky (my rabbit), Penny (my dog) and Soda (my guinea pig) all died and with each death the intense need to make everything perfect for the remaining ones increased. The regrets regarding what I perceived to be my failure's regarding their care haunted me daily and through vivid nightmares every night. These thoughts and feelings, combined with my failure to cope with or accept death and my determination to punish myself, contributed to my dangerous mindset.

Even before their deaths the destructive behaviours had started, I had this intense need not to be noticed, I felt I had nothing of worth to say and if anyone really knew me they wouldn't like me so it became essential to me that I was a small as possible. Losing weight was a way to disappear. Additionally, and it may seem strange for an anorexic to say, I don't hate food, there are certain foods I love (I crave pizza daily!) so in order to punish myself I decided that there were certain foods I was 'not allowed'. What I didn't realise then is that the anorexic mindset thrives on such decisions, clearly it was never going to stop at certain foods, very quickly it developed to not being allowed any food. I devised ways of monitoring my progress, for example, I wore a wide elastic belt with my school uniform and every week would cut a bit more of the belt off, if I had lost enough weight it would fit, if not then the belt would cut into me and hurt – either way I was achieving my aim.

After a while my parents and teachers at school began to notice, more specifically Mum saw my emaciated arms (in error I had worn a short sleeved nightshirt) and my school house head had phoned to say they were 'concerned' about me. They arranged for me to see an educational psychologist. All I can remember of the meeting were two things; the first was that he wore red socks (one of which had a hole in), and the second was that his opening words to me were 'well I thought you'd be all skin and bones but you don't look too bad at all'. My response to this 'encouraging' remark was to go away and lose another stone within a month.

My Mum then took me to our G.P; his attitude was one that is very common amongst G.Ps. In spite of every thing my Mum was telling him, about my weight loss, my obsessive behaviours, my reluctance to see a problem etc, he did not even weigh me. He did not even speak to me; he just looked at my Mum and said 'it will be interesting to see what Katharine is like in the summer holidays', clearly I just disliked school! I still find it absolutely remarkable that a huge number of the medical profession have so little knowledge or understanding of eating disorders. If he had properly intervened at that point, if he had had any inkling of the danger I was in, mentally and physically, he could have made such a difference. At the time of course, I was delighted, Mum had forced me to the doctors and he had effectively said that there was nothing wrong with me. Again, to my mind that meant I had to be left alone.

All the while my love for and obsession with my animals intensified, and although this later became a real difficulty, at age 15 it was this that saved my life for the first time. Mum told me that we would have to sell Pete (my pony) as I would soon be too weak to look after him and she wouldn't be able to do it as she'd be looking after me. The prospect of losing Pete was too horrific to bear, something extraordinary had been forged between us and I needed him. Although the bond with all my pets was intense - Pete got me away from the house, away from school, away from people. Not just physically away but mentally and emotionally I was whole when I was with him because nothing could frighten me quite so much. When Whisky died I went and sat in the field (as I have done numerous times) and just stared out feeling so much pain, such an abject failure (she was young when she died). Pete looked up from the other side of the field, stopped grazing and came straight towards me. I hadn't called him or even said anything out loud. He came right up close and rested his head on my shoulder and just stayed there. Without the need for words, without me doing anything, he knew I was hurting. He always knew and reacted to how I was feeling, not a single human knew the way he did. However powerful the illness, I knew that if I lost him (and in turn my sanctuary) I would be utterly lost for good.

I forced myself to start eating again, not a great deal of weight was gained but no more was lost and physically I was able to carry on. I realise this begs the question, if I could stop the intense starvation then, why could I not do so before? My only response to this is that it is a perfect example of how complex the illness is, it is not solely about food and weight, these are merely symptoms. I just developed other symptoms during that time. My mental and emotional state, were increasingly disturbed and, without the obvious weight loss, it was allowed to develop unchecked, unchallenged.

It was during the sixth form that the physical aspects of my illness increased again. I learnt what is, arguably, the most physically damaging behaviour an anorexic can learn, I learnt how to make myself sick, and to my cost became extremely good at it. This gave me the ability to lose weight, to hurt myself without people asking questions. If they saw me eating there couldn't be any reason to question me about my weight. I could eat anything and the punishment could come afterwards, to my thinking, the fact that inducing vomiting hurt was just an added bonus. I was still losing weight which was comforting to me and that could be covered with clothes, for a while any concerns anyone had disappeared.

And that was what I really wanted, to be left alone, to not be questioned, to just be with my animals and not have humans know me at all. My animals gave me a depth of security that I could not find elsewhere; when I was with any of them everything was so much better. Even 'A' level work was bearable so long as Soda was on my lap! Away from them the panic was constant; with them I felt safe and was able to relax. I talked to them about everything, they were the only ones who knew everything about me – what went on in my head, how I felt. The fact that they couldn't speak was part of the comfort, they couldn't tell anyone any of it and they still loved me regardless. With them I was never judged, I felt safe because I believed they would never stop loving me. My place with them was real and secure, I could hold on to them, they were mine and I was theirs. All the humans in my life felt unreliable, because if they really knew me, they wouldn't even like me, let alone love me.

I was not a total recluse however, as much as I would have liked to have been. I did have friends and a boyfriend but none of it was real to me. During evenings out, and sometimes during the school day, I would take myself somewhere away from people to thump a wall, just so I could feel the pain, just so I could feel something. Damaged, swollen knuckles I refused to do anything about were commonplace through sixth form and then university. I felt so out of absolutely every aspect of normal life but by hurting myself, punishing myself for being me, I could play my part in 'the human world' as I referred to it when talking to my animals (who were my solace and emotional outlet every day).

The only other real comfort I found away from my animals was through acting, it was the one thing I allowed myself to acknowledge I was good at, the one thing that I could do right. The appeal of course was that I was allowed to be someone else, it was necessary for me to be and I loved (still do love) the escapism, the time off from being me and from all the pressure in my head. In some ways I know it seems bizarre that I should hide so much from real life but be happy to put myself in the spotlight on stage, and yet I felt more real there than ever in 'real' life. For as long as I can remember, starting from a solo performance of Alice in Wonderland age 7, the need to perform, to be someone else, has been incredibly strong. Throughout my years at school, drama class and the school shows were the only times I felt really comfortable, bizarrely, the only time it was alright to be me, because I had the ability to be someone, anyone else.

I also found great strength through running, during the time when I was forcing myself to eat, running made it more bearable. To know that I was not only burning calories (and of course putting myself through pain to do so) but also that it was again something I could do. The only problem with an anorexic mindset, in this regard, is that even when it is acknowledged that the individual is achieving, it is never enough.

The need for perfection is often a common trait amongst anorexics (as mentioned previously), often it is inaccurately believed to be solely sought through academic achievements but in actual fact it can be absolutely anything. Nothing achieved is ever enough, no amount of success or achievement can ever measure up to the, self imposed, impossibly high standards.

Through the two years of sixth form my mental health deteriorated a great deal, my weight remained fairly stable although I was trapped in the damaging behaviour of only allowing myself to eat if it could be 'removed' afterwards. The real crisis for me came when the time approached to apply for university, I didn't want to go. Absolutely, categorically did not want to go, but I couldn't tell anyone. I tried, in the kind of round about never getting to the point way that people use when they are too cowardly to say what they really mean. The facts of the matter were that I did not want to leave Pete and Soda and I was totally terrified at the prospect of living away from home, although home was uncomfortable with constant tension and arguments, at least it was safe in the sense that it was familiar. I also believed I needed to be there to try and keep the peace between my parents, I believed that although it was unlikely I could make things better; at least I could stop it getting any worse. I went ahead with applications though as I didn't know how to tell the truth but I genuinely believed it wouldn't happen, surely my parents would realise how desperate I was to stay at home and would tell me it was o.k.

I love my parents deeply and at no point through our lives could they be described as 'pushy' but we have all grown up with the unspoken expectation that we achieve. They would say that they wanted us to have every opportunity, to me (I cannot speak for Nick and Helen) that was a constant pressure not to disappoint. I studied hard for my 'A' levels, but did not perform as I should as Soda died just a week before the first exam. I was often ridiculed whilst he was alive for my attachment to a guinea pig and therefore no one really understood my grief at his loss. He loved and trusted me totally unconditionally and allowed me to love him, I used to cuddle him endlessly and he never protested. I am extremely lucky to have had that. As mentioned previously, with the loss of each pet the intensity of feeling and need to look after the others increased as did the need not to make any mistakes. With Whisky, Penny and Soda I have deep regrets and guilt regarding things I did or didn't do, these stay with me to this day and guilt is one of my major triggers, a huge contributory factor to the strength of my illness.

And so with the death of Soda, only Pete was left and my already intensely strong attachment to him intensified, the thought of leaving him was too painful to accept. And yet I was offered places at universities and it was assumed that I was going, 'what else are you going to do?' 'You have to do something' etc these were the sorts of statements I received when I tried to explain to my parents that I couldn't go. I was gripped with an intense, overwhelming fear I could not disappoint them by going against what they believed I should do. By this time I was utterly convinced that if they really knew me, if they knew how bad and evil I was, they wouldn't love me and if I gave further disappointment then it would seal the justification for not loving or even liking me at all. Without them loving me, I knew I was finished.

I have since tried to blame them for making me go, but they truly believed it was the right thing for me, they were concerned regarding my attachment to Pete and the fact that I showed hardly any sign of a life away from him, a life amongst humans. They also believed me to be intelligent and that I should make the most of that intelligence by developing a career. What they didn't know, of course, was how ill I was, how much I depended on Pete for survival (this is no exaggeration), how scared I was of everything and how dangerous it would be for me to be away.

I cannot blame them for this, I couldn't find the words to tell them, obviously they knew I was messed up – often during explosive rows Dad would claim to know psychiatrists he was going to send me to (he never did anything about it and I don't even know if he genuinely knew anyone or not!). I remember one row in particular my Mum said to Dad 'Katharine struggles to cope with life' I really wish they had realised how much. My thinking was so deluded and I was so desperate to make them proud that I could not risk disappointing them, and so I took the place at Cambridge and I went.

It was the biggest mistake of my life; I sank into the worst depression I had ever experienced up until that point. The pain I experienced being away from Pete and away from home was immense, it was just too impossible to bear but I knew I couldn't leave. Trapped in an environment that was totally wrong for me, away from everything that made me feel safe and saved me from myself, I still have absolutely no idea how I survived those four years. The word 'safe' is one that was used in hospital a great deal, at first I thought it was nonsense, I had no idea what they meant by it – I do now. It is true to say that living within the depths of anorexia is truly a living hell. It is like drowning,

47

drowning under the wave of intense negative thought and emotion from which there is no relief, even happy, positive moments in life are clouded by the inner turmoil. The illness totally takes over, reading the diary I kept during my time at university it is incredible how irrational my thoughts were and yet how real.

Suicidal thoughts had always been present with me for as long as I could remember but being at university made it a very real possibility. I just couldn't cope with anything, I couldn't make friends because I couldn't face people, anyone who has experienced a panic attack will know the fear is all consuming, panic attacks became a daily occurrence – my degree class may have been higher if I'd not had to leave so many lectures!

I also developed a very fixed routine regarding food, if I ate anything I had to be sick afterwards but at home (the weekends I was allowed home – apparently it was not good for me to come every weekend, yet another thing I should have spoken out against) I ate 'normally'. In my diary, I wrote 'I must be so careful at home, they must not know my methods'. It was so calculated, so flawlessly planned that it is little wonder that no-one had any idea what was wrong with me.

A college lecturer once called me into her office to reprimand me for my behaviour – apparently I was either high as a kite or incredibly low and it was affecting the balance in the group! In truth my behaviour was erratic, if I was succeeding in starvation or was due to go home I would become the performer, making people laugh etc but if not then the depression would be obvious. At no point, however, did this lecturer or anyone else think to ask me what was wrong, or if I was o.k. Although my parents were left in no doubt that I was deeply unhappy they couldn't possibly have known how bad things were. Even I had no idea how bad it was going to get.

During the first two terms of my fourth year things actually improved, I was running again and so allowing myself to eat more, I met Andy who remains one of the only people in the world whom I truly trust and am genuinely close too and I was on the home stretch – within months the 'sentence' would be over and I would be home. In the Easter holidays however, just 2 months before finals, Pete died. He had become absolutely everything to me and I have always described him as carrying all the good in me. I was the person I wanted to be when I was with him, the connection a human can have with a horse is extraordinary and I still feel so privileged that I had that. Pete could read my moods, he knew how I felt and with him I was safe – my madness (I frequently refer to it as that now, it somehow makes it sound less dangerous) couldn't consume me when I was in my field with him.

Two years before he died I had got a little mare from the International League for Protection of Horses as a companion for him called Trixie, after he died I spent hours and hours in the field trying to feel the comfort I'd always felt and trying to keep her company. Even though I knew that I couldn't give her the same company as a pony I felt I had to have some worth somewhere, I should have been able so save Pete – or more to the point I should never have left him to go to university.

The truth is, of course, that I could not have saved him, we had him operated on but he was just too old, his body too tired, to make it through the recovery. As I stood with him in that stable in Newmarket and watched him die I felt my soul die too, I loved him and was so deeply damaged already that losing the one thing I was sure of, the one thing that kept me alive and the last real link to the others, was just too much for my head to reconcile. To this day I still feel the hole I felt on that day, I doubt if it will ever be filled.

Following his death my health (both mental and physical) plummeted, it was two weeks before I was due to run the London Marathon and I couldn't eat, sleep or train. I had a huge amount of sponsorship resting on my completing the run and yet I had no idea how to do anything. Mum persuaded me to try and go ahead with the race and see it as being for Pete, I know that she hoped it would be cathartic and would help pull me through. It didn't, I ran the race and it remains one of my proudest moments but the illness had a hold like never before and once the marathon was done, I really believed it would kill me. I was marching headlong towards my own destruction and although I could see it, I was absolutely powerless to stop it.

It is impossible for me to fully recount that last term at university, I cannot remember a lot of it clearly. When Pete was dying I promised him that I would finish my degree – at the time I felt that leaving him had to result in something, and that I would take care of Trixie, it became essential to me that I fulfill those promises. Also for the first time ever I didn't want to be at home, even though I desperately wanted to be close to Trixie it was just so painful to be there, having to go back to Cambridge was a brief relief.

Unfortunately of course, if pain is inside you it goes with you wherever you go. Andy was an enormous support to me, as were Louise and Chelli (friends who I had met through Andy) but they couldn't really reach me and anyway, they had their own exams to study for, for so much of the time I was alone with my head that tortured me mercilessly.

There was one night in particular which I cannot believe I lived through, in my darkest moments since I have often said I should have died that night. I got very drunk (alcohol had become an escape route) and ended up in the middle of the college playing fields screaming and shouting. To begin with it was just at anyone, anything that could hear me, then it was at God – it was so loud that lads from the accommodation block came running out with hockey sticks as they thought someone was being attacked! Later one of them told me he had never heard so much pain, I have often felt like I could scream forever and never release all the pain. At the time I genuinely believed that Pete had been taken from me as a punishment for being evil, that no matter how much I punished myself, God would always want to punish me more. I'm not even sure I believe in God but that night I did and I believed that the punishment would never end; the only way to stop it would be to end my own existence totally.

I thought I had felt suicidal before but that night, with the confines of rational thought removed I desperately needed death with intensity I had never felt before. It is like falling through never ending darkness, drowning in an all engulfing wave of hopeless searing pain that will never be alleviated. There is no one who can help, nothing that can make any of it right and no reason, absolutely no reason at all to keep up the pretence of a life. I did not deserve anyone or anything, I was evil, twisted to my rotten core and so unworthy of love that I was destined to lose anything that I loved. I didn't deserve love so all those I loved would be taken from me, my ultimate punishment for being the person I was. My own death is not something that frightens me (still doesn't) and suicide was the best solution to the mess I had created, an end to all of it, an end to being me.

Any thoughts of my family (the reason I had never been selfish enough to go through with it before) were quickly dismissed by the prominent belief that they would be better off without me and I was so evil I didn't deserve them anyway.   I self harmed that night, the only time in all my years with the illness and although I intended the cutting to result in my death it actually saved my life. The pain of the initial (not major) cuts broke through the drunken barrier to rationality and the something deep inside that has always stopped me going though with it woke up. I can picture myself now as I sank to the floor of the corridor outside my room and cried until I just couldn't cry anymore. I managed to call Nick and after talking to him, collapsed on my bed and slept.

The next day I had to carry on. Finals were only three weeks away and if I had to live, I had to keep my promises. I have never allowed myself to get drunk since, in fact I barely touch alcohol at all (the most is a shandy made when my husband has a lager which is so weak we call it flavoured lemonade!). It is far too dangerous for me.

It is remarkable to me that Andy and Louise stuck by me through that term, I have thanked them since but I don't think I will ever be able to thank them enough. I sat my finals and got my degree, not the class I wanted, another failure to the list in my view. The fact that I had a degree from Cambridge was totally irrelevant to me; it was not good enough because it was not the degree class I had decided I should get.

And so the sentence at university was over but going home was nothing like as it should have been, in fact I was so messed up that I began to realise that I was losing the ability to really feel anything except intense disgust for myself and a huge gaping hole inside. I loved my family, Trixie and Sasha (the family dog my parents got two years after Penny died, who I like to think of as mine!) but I felt so lost, I couldn't relate to my family properly my solace came through Trixie and Sasha although being in the field where Pete should have been was so deeply painful.

Through the summer months after graduation, it became clear to everyone that I had to receive treatment, real treatment or after over 10 years of battling the physical aspects of the illness and a lifetime of living with the mental ones, I would lose, the illness would win once and for all. I managed to work as a teacher for two terms, first full time then reduced to part time but by Easter 1998 it had become impossible to work at all.

Through my G.P (a much more well informed and helpful one than before) I was referred to the eating disorders service, part of general psychiatry, at the local hospital. To be perfectly honest this was an absolute waste of time, both for me and the health service. It was arranged that I would meet with a psychologist once a week and they assigned me to a lady who was still in training. Whilst I understand that they have to complete case studies etc, it was totally ridiculous to give a hardened anorexic like myself to someone without any experience. It is true to say that I was not really ready to engage properly in any kind of therapy but she had no idea how to begin talking to me. For example, the first thing she did was give me a selection of questionnaires to fill in – anorexics lie! They lie about their behaviours (particularly regarding food, which most of these questionnaires were about), deception is a key part of the disturbed thinking and, having lived within the illness so long, I had become so proficient at it that there was no way anyone without real experience would know how to see through/get round that.

It was then agreed that I would meet with a consultant psychiatrist instead, I was under her 'care' for over 6 months during which time I deteriorated massively. She was an experienced psychiatrist but again she had no experience of dealing with eating disorders – she gave me many amusing memories however, for example the time she helpfully told me that 'if only you could shake off this anorexia you'd have a very bright future' and she also told me that I could be 'almost beautiful'!? Whilst weekly appointments can undoubtedly make a difference to some people, I would certainly not recommend it as beneficial for the sufferer or economically sound for the N.H.S. From a personal point of view I found it deeply damaging to spend an hour trying to talk about serious issues only to be sent home to cope on my own with the feelings those issues brought up. My way of dealing with negative emotion was to punish myself; weekly therapy simply increased the necessity for punishment.

I lost more weight and I again began to focus on suicide as the only option, this time, to try and remove the guilt, I even tried to convince my Mum that they would all be better off without me.

A real breakthrough came when my sister saw an article in the local paper for an inpatient clinic in Norwich (just 45 minutes from home), she did a lot of research on it and an assessment was arranged. As soon as I arrived I knew that those people would be able to help me, they understood what I was talking about (at least they certainly gave the impression they did) and realised that I was seriously ill and recommended that I was admitted and treated as soon as possible.

The catch was, that it was technically a private clinic (although there were a number of NHS patients there at the time) and we would need to apply for NHS funding, to secure this we needed the support of my psychiatrist. To begin with she said she would support this, and then we heard nothing. She wouldn't take phone calls, or respond to the letters written by my Mum, my Dad and my sister. By this time I was so deeply depressed I was not able to see anyone other than my family and I also felt that my psychiatrist had totally let me down and so stopped keeping my appointments.

Eventually, after approximately two months of waiting, I received a letter quoting policy and stating that they would only ever make a referral to a recognised NHS unit and only in cases where the condition of 'the patient' was deemed to be life threatening. When my mum queried this statement she was told that my body weight was not low enough, this was in spite of the fact that I was nearly three stone underweight and, more importantly, my most recent blood test had shown dangerously low levels of potassium – in short my liver was in trouble. Additionally my psychiatrist knew better than anyone that I was genuinely suicidal, therefore it beggars belief that my condition could not be considered life threatening. Basically the reality of eating disorders is not recognised by general areas of the NHS, the seriousness of the illness is simply measured by the sufferer's body weight. Dangerous behaviours regarding food can be carried out without the individual actually losing very much weight or even looking particularly ill.

This weight based criteria totally ignores the internal affects of malnutrition, even when maintaining a reasonable weight, let alone the daily anguish punctuated by suicidal thoughts and often leading to the actual act. One in twenty sufferers will die as a result of their illness (more than all other mental illnesses put together). I had seriously deteriorated during out patient treatment, and yet, in spite of these facts, it was considered that I was not in need of an inpatient treatment programme.

After another couple of months of my parents frantic letter writing and calls to anyone they could think of, miraculously I was given an assessment date for a place in an inpatient unit in London. Thanks only to the persistence of my parents I was finally going to be seen by specialist at an NHS eating disorders unit, it really disturbs me as to what would have happened to me if I hadn't had parents who were articulate enough to really argue my case. Without their insistence that I needed real treatment we would never have even known that the unit existed, let alone have been referred for assessment. By the time I went for my assessment at the beginning of December 1998 I had been in the depths of the illness, the most serious bout of my life, for 20 months! I still maintain that in financial and practical terms I would have been so much more economical to treat if all that time had not been wasted, the deeper into the illness a person is and the lower the weight/greater the physical complications, the longer and more in depth the treatment needs to be.

At the assessment, again because they were specialists and experienced, they recognised the seriousness of my condition and wanted to admit me as soon as a bed became available. During the assessment, the nurse asked me if I was sure about treatment I replied 'I have no choice', she said 'of course you do, this is totally up to you' for the only time during that interview I looked her right in the eye 'no there is no choice, I do this or this thing will kill me'.

The stakes were really that high, life or death situations come in different forms, that moment in my life was mine. I was admitted a month later on January 25th 1999 and started a treatment programme which was to last 10 months.

During Treatment ...

Diary entry – Monday 25th January 1999

'Standing on the edge of a cliff you are faced with choices, you can either turn back to safety, move forward and allow yourself to fall or choose to jump. My cliff didn't give me such straight forward choices, in order to reach safety I had to give myself into the hands of others and fight my way back. My other option was to stay balanced precariously just waiting to fall, or jump if the waiting to fall became too much to bear. Not much of a choice to a real person but for me, with my messed up head, I had to fight the will to go on precariously balancing. Fortunately for my better side, for those who love me, my animals who need me and my own desperate wish for a real life made me decide to at least try and fight my way to safety... I cannot really write about today, leaving Trixie and Sasha caused a pain I have never experienced before it were as though I was abandoning the last shred of my decent real self. I feel I've failed them and consequently myself... I've always needed my animals to keep me together, to carry the better side of me, I desperately wanted to avoid letting them down but what if I became more and more ill, what use would I be then ... I've pushed them (Mum and Dad) to the limit I hate the illness and myself for causing such hurt, worry and frustration ... they both deserve happiness, and a break from me. I'm so scared, so isolated, I don't understand how I got here, I want Trix, Sash, Mum and Dad. I want to go home.'

I can vividly remember that day, I can picture all of it, every moment – I believe there really are things that stay with you forever. I do not wish to spend too long describing the hospital environment, thankfully for those in treatment now the unit has moved to a vastly improved premises and consequently the facilities are incomparably better and I'm sure more conducive to recovery.

Suffice it to say that the building itself is indelibly imprinted on my memory, and the fact that the floor was shared with general psychiatry (eating disorders at one end, everything from depressives to paranoid schizophrenics at the other) gave me totally unique experiences. For example, there was a paranoid schizophrenic who singled out one of the girls on the ward, Chloe, as the person who was 'after her' and the way to protect herself was to throw water over Chloe every time she saw her. It was deeply disturbing that the majority of the patients were there simply because no one had any idea what else to do with them, there was virtually no real treatment beyond medication and the feeling of hopelessness was palpable.

The eating disorders end of the ward was a very different story, over time I discovered that there was great support between patients but when I first arrived I was absolutely horrified, I had never witnessed other people with the illness before, for several weeks the physical manifestation of what raged in my head was too much to take.

Diary Entry – Thursday 28th January 1999

'There is so much pain here; I simply cannot describe it well enough. As I write this I can hear heart wrenching crying from the room next door, even with my walkman on I can't block it out. The truly terrifying thing is that even when the pain isn't audible you can see it. About half of the patients here are virtually skeletal, they are so wasted, I can't look at them, even through clothes you can see the outline of their sharp protruding bones. They represent Anorexia as

everyone on the outside perceives it – gaunt faces, staring eyes and <u>so</u> thin even when they smile it looks ghoulish... I can't bare all the pain, my own was bad enough but seeing this, it's like some kind of nightmare ...'

On arrival I was asked to sign a contract which included agreeing to consume all the food and drink given, it also included accepting all instructions from the 'team' (consisting of doctors, nurses, psychotherapists and occupational therapists), I signed it willingly as for the first time in my life I had reached the point where I was really scared of the illness. An anorexic will not engage in therapy to reach recovery unless they have reached the very bottom and recognise that the illness is controlling them and will kill them if they do not really fight it, if they do not allow people to help them fight it. That was where I was on admission.

The first week it was something of a baptism by fire, the term used by the staff was to 'hit the ground running' but I think my description is a rather more accurate depiction! I was set a target weight and put on the weight gain diet which in real terms means 3000 calories a day and a huge amount of fluid, the amount of tea one person can consume is really extraordinary!

There are arguments that this approach is not appropriate, it is a huge amount to ask of any eating disorders patient. The view of the hospital was that the anorexic mindset cannot be bargained with; the decisions have to be absolute and the action total. I know this is absolutely the case. I do not believe, however, it helps to foster a love of food! Some foods became absolutely loathsome, especially in the case of custard creams when having faced 9 a day for weeks. The very sight of them on a supermarket shelf is simply too much!

Physically, the pain of consuming such huge amounts of food was excruciating, stomachs shrink during starvation and the ability to digest food is compromised. Clearly it is only a matter of time for the body to adjust but it seems like an eternity. There is also an extremely bizarre physical process called thermogenesis which occurs when the metabolism is suddenly kick started and has to go into overdrive to burn up the fuel being provided. What this actually feels like is that you are going to spontaneously combust! For the first time in years I was hot, to the point where in January I was walking around wearing a vest top and shorts. The hospital was kept very, very warm as so many patients were at a dangerously low weight but for those of us on the recovery programme it was uncomfortable to say the least!

Whilst trying to cope physically with the affects of eating again, there was of course the mental strain; the guilt for me was overwhelming.

Diary entry – Tuesday 26th January 1999
'I cried over my supper, it was so huge and they made me eat it alone I don't want to face piles of food alone. I don't hate food – I just don't allow myself it, I need to be told 'you must eat or we won't help you' and 'you can eat, it's ok' I want to be forced, then it's not my fault.'

I did it though, regardless of guilt or panic. I had to trust them that it was what I needed to be doing. When I made the decision to accept treatment I decided I had to be 100% committed to it, I knew nothing less could work. There were four types of treatment programme in the unit and after initial assessments every patient was given a specific diagnosis. Some patients were there on what was called the 'safe weight programme' which basically meant that they were not ready to engage in therapy and so were simply there until their weight raised sufficiently to take them out of immediate physical danger. One of the girls I was sharing a room with had been admitted 12 times on that basis.

I was diagnosed as impulsive anorexic, the distinction was made regarding the behaviours which were engaged in – the main difference between the two anorexic programmes, for me, was the fact that I induced vomiting.

There was a great deal of cross over between the two anorexic programmes and for some therapy groups we were altogether.

We were also brought together (including those admitted on the safe weight programme) for the somewhat bizarre phenomenon of 'social group'. Given the mix of people and the struggle we were all going through it very often did not work as intended! The first half hour would be spent in silence as we were meant to suggest what we wanted to do and no one had the confidence to speak. The most surreal week occurred when it was (eventually) decided that we should play Jenga (the game which involves a tower of building blocks and each player removes a block until the tower falls), most of the group were critically underweight and therefore had the shakes. I find Jenga generally works best with a steady hand!

The treatment programme, which consisted of individual work (depending on specific need) and group work – art therapy, life skills etc, was both amazing and terrifying; basically the team break you down into little pieces and then put you back together as a whole person without the behaviours and in control of the illness. Early in my treatment someone said to me that I had to keep fighting because 'things are happening even when you don't realise it', I found myself saying the same thing to a group on my last day before discharge.

The process is agonising though and from very early into the programme, nothing makes any sense and I totally lost sight of who I was.

Diary Entry – Tuesday 9th February 1999
'…during ward round it was like watching myself drown, the image of me growing smaller and smaller as my voice grew fainter and fainter. Something happened to me today, I lost part of me, I lost my hope… the numbness, the headache and sick feeling, the intolerable loneliness and the immeasurable despair. I want to cry but the tears stop just

short of choking me, I don't know what to do, how to think, nothing feels right and I'm really scared of myself.'

When living in the illness it defined me, all my thoughts, all my feelings and the consequent behaviours were governed by my seriously disturbed thinking. I literally had no idea how to deal with anything in a real, rational, normal way. For the first time in my life I had to face the things that hurt me and allow them to really hurt, just emotionally without moving to physical punishment on myself.

As time progressed I reluctantly had to accept that yes, the symptoms of the illness do serve a purpose, my behaviours over the years have allowed me to avoid really facing and dealing with the things that scared me and damaged me so deeply. I had thought that I was grieving for my animals, I thought I was reconciled to my parents dreadful marriage and divorce, I really believed I had blocked out the other things that had happened and had left me with the belief that I was so evil, so unworthy of real life – I had never really dealt with any of it. I had relied on the illness induced behaviours to keep me going, if I was punishing myself I could go on living, but of course I hadn't really been living at all.

The reality of the low points was truly horrific; the majority of people admitted on the recovery programme discharge themselves or break the contract and are asked to leave, well before the end. For several months the need to run away home and hide was enormous but something, something deep inside kept pushing me forward.

This was in spite of the fact that, at times, events on the ward were so surreal it was hard to keep any grip on reality, many times in my diary I described existence on the ward as an 'alternate universe' where normality had no place. For example, there was John (from the general psychiatry ward) who without any warning would get up from watching television and ring the fire alarm, as it was a hospital the direct link to the fire station meant that three engines would show up, seemingly instantaneously. Bizarrely, John would show absolutely no reaction to this whatsoever, indeed after ringing the alarm he would calmly resume watching television. Also two men informed me that there were a load of heads and brains in a shed and the doctors do experiments on people and 'turn them inside out with drugs'!

The most surreal and utterly bizarre event occurred when one Saturday afternoon was spent in the common room with patients from both wards watching One Flew Over The Cuckoo's Nest. I sat there watching and it slowly dawned that there was something very wrong in watching that particular film in that environment! I had to stop watching when about 45 minutes into the film several people got up and went to queue for their medication!

Without a doubt the aspect of treatment which both helped keep me on the programme and saved my life was the individual psychotherapy, my psychotherapist was extraordinary in her ability to figure me out and challenge me to face up to and work things through until issues reached a point where I could deal with them, or at the very least accept them. Some sessions I couldn't talk at all, other times I talked as though I could never say enough, she was able to take whatever I said, no matter how much or how little and help me to see the reality of things. For the first time ever, there began to be some clarity to my thoughts, the violent thoughts of self loathing were less intense, the nightmares I had experienced so vividly for years began to ease and I started to allow myself the belief that I could be well.

I was totally unprepared for what happened about half way through the programme; suddenly I hit what can only be described as a wall. For the first few months of treatment, although I struggled being away from home, having to eat, beginning to engage in therapy, finding the confidence to speak out in groups etc I very quickly became caught up in a kind of euphoric hope – these people understood, these people could help me get rid of this 'thing', I would be cured and have and normal happy life etc, etc.

That belief really was madness.

Without any warning I woke up one day and was consumed by an overwhelming depression and a total wish to just give up. I had no idea who I was, without the behaviours everything was just too raw, too real and it was horrifically terrifying. I had no idea who I was, how to relate to people, what to think about anything or what on earth I was going to do with the rest of my life. I believed at that point that life with me in control and not the illness was just impossible, I was not strong enough and never would be.

Diary Entry – Monday May 31st *1999*
'I can't bear feeling like this, it's utterly dreadful and I can't describe it but whatever this feeling is, I can't live with it. They go on and on about opening up and talking but I don't know how anymore, if I knew how I wouldn't know what to say. I'm so desperate for help and I'm scared of myself but being well seems such an unattainable goal, I don't know if I'll make it … I'm simply not coping'.

Thankfully hospital was the safest environment to have such a crisis as I was put on 10 minute observations (suicide watch) and after a few days of not being able to speak properly to anyone I met with the doctor and was prescribed anti-depressants. It is very important to note that this is the only time when I would advocate taking anti-depressants at all; they must be used in conjunction with therapy. Alone they are merely a plaster over an infected wound – masking the damage but actually worsening the situation in the long term. The doctor said to me that it was simply to get me back to a level where I could engage in therapy again and talk about what was going on in my head – without it, relapse and removal from the programme would probably have been inevitable. It was possible to take a 'time out' which was a week at home to think about whether the treatment is really what you want or not – I did not consider this to be an option, if I had gone home (however much I wanted to) I would have been totally lost, the suicide I had staved off for so long would have actually happened, of this I have no doubt.

The reason I mention this period is to prepare and reassure anyone going into treatment, even when it appears that you are making real headway, the affect of the illness on the brain is extraordinary and there will be times when any sort of recovery seems utterly impossible. For several other patients during my time on the ward, these crisis points did result in full relapse and discharge, the girl I had been sharing a room with was at a lower point when they discharged her than she had been on admission. She should have been moving on to the day patient phase of the programme but the fear of being 'out there' had been too strong a trigger for the anorexia.

Diary Entry – Tuesday 6th April 1999
'The ward fell apart today, 3 discharges including Katie which was an unbelievable shock, I share a room with her and I didn't realise it had gone so wrong. She had been water loading (to falsify weight) and restricting for over a month …it's all so bizarre, last weekend she was off on weekend leave all healthy and positive acting. I can't believe her lies were so convincing, anorexia has an incredible force – it is easy to underestimate it.'

I guess in a way it was good for me to be on the receiving end of an anorexics deception, it also brought home to me how easy it would be to slip right back. Something I could not afford to do.

Somehow, I came through that time, I'm not even sure how. There was no specific moment where I suddenly felt better but through the continued therapy and the drive not to give up I somehow started to move forwards again.

As difficult as this period was it proved to me that I had untold inner strength, previously I considered myself to be so weak and pathetic, why couldn't I get myself well etc but after that crisis point in hospital I realised that I was stronger than I had ever imagined.

This helped the latter stages of the programme enormously, not that it was easy, there were further crisis points but I was able to keep using therapy properly and so instead of moving backwards I was able to move on. This was essential, as accepting the changing practicalities of the programme was challenging enough.

Throughout the course of the programme, increased freedom was given, starting with total confinement to the unit, building gradually through a 5 minute walk in the grounds to free afternoons to go into town and then increasing to overnight then weekend leave. For the final 5 months, I was treated as a day patient, living at the YMCA but in hospital 9 am to 5 pm Monday to Friday.

Although going to hospital each day was not quite the same as going to work it did provide that kind of structure and it felt a little more like real life. This was helped by the fact that YMCAs are much flashier establishments than I ever imagined!

During the day patient phase I actually stopped hating myself and began to accept that being me was really not so bad. It was such a colossal relief to no longer feel the need to fight with myself, the illness seemed to have gone and I believed that I was cured, I was even happy with how I was looking – another lifetime first! The euphoria I had felt during the early stages of treatment had returned with even more conviction. As I approached the end of my day patient treatment I really believed that feeling, if I felt like that at the end of treatment it surely had to be real.

I completed my treatment and in October 1999 I was discharged and came home. Without a doubt those nine months in hospital saved my life. When I thanked the staff in my final ward round, the words sounded so futile, no matter what I had said, I could never really tell them what they'd done for me.

Initially the euphoria came with me and being home, especially being able to look after Trixie and Sasha, was amazing, it was as though I was seeing everything through new eyes. For a while I had no fear about being out of hospital (i.e. leaving that level of support) as I believed I was better.

The treatment programme continued to a certain extent in the form of attending an outpatient group with a further six weeks of individual therapy. I found the travelling each week very stressful however and really felt that the outpatients group was not of value to me, so after the 6 weeks of therapy I discharged myself fully from the hospital system. For many I am sure that the weekly group would be excellent support but this particular group could not work for me as all the other members had completed the restrictive anorexic programme and it seemed that their thinking still focused a great deal on food related issues. Additionally the group facilitator was extraordinarily unpleasant to me in only the second week and this was really not the kind of support I needed.

It could be argued that to reject the weekly group was an error. In the months that followed I remained well but without access to people in the same position it was often hard to know what it was that I was meant to expect. However I am not sure that the stress of travelling and the difficult mix in the group would have answered those questions.

What did become very clear, after several months back home, was that I my view of my recovery had been totally deluded. The euphoria had felt wonderful and I have often wished since that it had been real. With hindsight I was being very foolish, it was hope that drove the belief and the need to believe. Whilst there is nothing wrong with hope, had I been even a little more realistic I now know my time since discharge would have been easier.

Since Treatment ...

Life in recovery with this illness is in so many ways even harder than life in the depths of the illness. The daily battle continues, in fact it is tougher than ever before. I came out of hospital looking so physically well and behaving as though I was totally better that it was so hard to reconcile that with how scared I still was. The only way I can describe the experience is like being a child in an adult's body, with an adult life and adult responsibilities. I had spent all my adolescent years consumed by the illness, the behaviours got me through daily life and now I was back out in the world without them – it was like free falling without a parachute.

Every day (even now) I am learning how to cope with the real world in a real way, the temptation to hide away and not do so is enormous, it is true to say that everything involves hard work. I faced a massive crisis point, and my most powerful trigger, when Trixie died in January 2001 (she was 31). In the years after Pete's death she had become invaluable to me, she had totally transformed for a nervous, distant character into the most affectionate pony I have ever had the privilege to encounter. The pain of losing her, which also meant that my life revolving around ponies was gone too, was horrendous and to allow myself to grieve, accept the pain and work through the loss was something I had never faced before without the behaviours to take the focus.

As mentioned previously I have had to accept that the behaviours had a definite use, as well as being my means of punishment, they were also a means of survival. The temptation to allow all the pain to go into them after Trixie's death was incredibly strong. I really, really struggled and was terrified that I was experiencing a relapse; I thought the illness was back and I would end up just as desperately low as I was before.

What I had to accept then and I have been working on ever since is the fact that the illness is ever present but I can control it, however hard it is, especially at times of real trauma, I have to keep controlling it.

There have been many positive things, the most significant being marrying Steve on 1st June 2001 (the most perfect wedding day in all history). I met him during the day patient phase of treatment when Andy and I went to Chelli's wedding, I knew immediately he was the man I would marry. It still seems miraculous to me that after everything I am married. He is the most amazing, perfect man and an enormous support to me. If I ever need reasons outside of myself to keep fighting this illness I just look at him – I must have got that lucky for a reason!

In spite of such wonderful positives, life in recovery can be incredibly hard, the days when it all seems just too much, when I am just too tired of the fight that allowing it to take me seems very appealing. However, I have so much that has gone right for me since treatment, so much to hold on to and believe in, and none of it could have happened if I had simply given up.

I have become very realistic and philosophical over the past year, I am now in my fourth year of recovery and I think it takes this long to gain real perspective on the illness. I now have clarity of thought to acknowledge that whilst I may struggle, by rights, I should have been dead years ago and yet I made it this far. There has to be a reason for that, there has to be some purpose to my life even though I don't know it yet. I just have to allow myself time to find out – and it really doesn't't matter how long it takes.

It would be so easy to fall into the self piteous 'why me', 'I didn't ask to be born with this' thinking, but I refuse to succumb to that. The facts are that I was born with this but I am also so lucky in so many ways that I would be crazy in the truest sense if I ever ignored the positive life I can live.

I try to allow myself the bad days though, it i important through recovery that I acknowledge and acc, how I'm feeling. I always try hard to make sure that there is something positive to take from everyday, however small that thing may be. Doing so makes surviving the bad days a little easier.

Awareness of behaviours is also absolutely imperative because the use of them can slip in so easily. I would love to be able to say that issues regarding food are completely resolved but unfortunately they are not and I am not sure they ever really will be. I have no idea about portion sizes, for other people or myself – it is a standing joke in our house that whenever I cook we should invite the neighbours since there is always more than enough food to go round! I also have very real trouble spending money on food, I hate it and feel that I don't deserve to spend money on something that could just make me fat whilst there are people in the world starving (I am now aware that this is irrational but I frequently need reminding). I very rarely allow myself what I would call treats (chocolate, cake etc) and if I do Steve has to eat half of it with me. I still cannot tolerate the feeling of being full, it frightens me intensely and so I try to eat several small meals - it feels safer that way.

Obsessive behaviours are still in evidence with me the latest being that all cooking utensils are spotlessly clean (to ensure there is no trace of meat on any of them) I have virtually stopped eating out through fear that restaurants will not be careful enough with the vegetarian food. The arguments that rage in my head between the rational and irrational thoughts are truly bizarre; as soon as I think a rational thought (or someone else says it out loud) the irrational negative one jumps straight in! Often it becomes such a muddle in my head that I feel genuine panic about what to do, how to make it stop. Unfortunately the only way to totally stop this particular obsession would be to just not eat, which is the option I have to fight against. Steve often tells me my head is tricking me (and it can feel just like that) which helps me counteract the irrational thoughts, seeing it as a 'thing' again in such circumstances can help! I know eventually rationality will win out over this new obsession because I know how to make sure it does now. It just takes time to work each new thing through.

There are other issues I still have to work on too, the most major of these being my self confidence. It is important for me to accept who I am, the self loathing I thought I had left in hospital is actually still with me but it is less venomous than it used to be, and the aim is to get rid of it altogether. I have spent the last 4 years of life in recovery still gauging my worth on my position with others and how others perceive me. I also still find it impossibly hard to let my family live their own lives, and I find it difficult to be away from Steve, my parents and our dogs.

My independence also really needs to improve, and I have to keep working to make sure that they do. It is simply not fair on Steve to have to look after me, which I have to say he does brilliantly, and has done since we met, but that is not the way it should be. I have to learn to depend on me – as well as on those around me.

It is vital that I take great care not to allow myself to believe that any of my behaviours are acceptable and beyond my control. No behaviour is beyond my control if I apply what I learnt in hospital and draw on all my inner resolve, strength that I never knew was there until I realised that my life depended on it.

All sufferers of eating disorders have this strength, it takes enormous strength to survive with the illness, it is essential to accept that and use that strength to fight. I would never for a single second suggest that this is easy, there are days when I feel that I am the weakest person in the world and the fight is beyond me. The truth is the daily fight is exhausting, Steve frequently finds me crying and has to listen to me say I can't do it any more. I get so totally exhausted and overwhelmingly frustrated with being me, with the struggle, with the constant difficulties and my bizarre thought processes.

And yet, even when I truly believe I am done fighting and the illness has to win, every bad day ends and the next day starts with new resolve because I am still alive, in the truest sense and whilst I am the illness is not winning. I really am a work in progress and facing these issues when I still feel so incredibly fragile is a challenge to say the least. I constantly face situations which make me feel nervous, uncomfortable and often overwhelmingly panicked but the key point now is that I do face them, as me, without behaviours to hide behind.

In hospital I was told that if I remained behaviour free for 2 years then I would never go back to those behaviours, unfortunately I do not agree with this at all. Even now I am still pulled towards my behaviours regarding food, particularly vomiting and I have slipped up a number of times since hospital. I know that I could be right back where I was incredibly quickly. On the occasions it has happened I have had to forgive myself and then reinforce all the reasons I must avoid such things. I have certainly not remained totally behaviour free and I think it was naïve to believe that I would be able to tackle real life and not experience the need for them. This does not mean that the use of behaviours is ok and I cannot allow myself to think of it as such.

As mentioned previously it is the awareness and acceptance that is essential. There was a huge amount done right in hospital and my time there saved my life, but I still have concerns that they did not really understand the *true* nature of the illness. If they had I wish they had relayed some of it to me so that I would have been better prepared for life in recovery.

My physical health is still a problem; general exhaustion, head aches, stomach pains (including digestive problems), joint pains and muscular tiredness are a regular occurrence (even when I haven't done anything really physical), which all irritate me beyond measure. My skin is thinner than it should be, it looks like old lady skin on my legs in particular, the veins down my thighs are so visible that they look rather like an impressive waterway! I don't heal quickly or well if I am bruised or cut, the slightest burn or scratch will scar me. Also it appears as though I have absolutely no natural body temperature – if it is below 25 degrees I am cold. Getting the temperature in our house right to keep me warm without making Steve expire is very tricky! I know, however, that I am lucky, although irritating, these are minor problems and appear to be the only physical legacy of years and years of malnutrition.

Indeed, I have managed a small amount of running again, something during hospital I never thought would happen. I really thought I had done my body far too much damage and it would never regain the strength to run as I demand – jogging just will not do! Over this summer in particular (after 4 years at target weight) running with my brother was the best running I have ever done, it has been really good to enjoy running without the ridiculous amount of pressure I used to enforce. Of course it takes huge mind over matter, although my muscle definition is improving, it feels as though I have top layer of muscle without any density to it. Patience is not my strong point but I do realise I have to allow by muscle to build and develop. Mind you, having wasted my leg muscle to nothing it is really miraculous that they will even hold me up, let alone do anything!

Even I have to acknowledge the huge progress I have made, the most significant of these being that I am totally honest with Steve, about everything. I have even told him immediately after I made myself sick the times it has happened. This is something totally new for me, as mentioned previously deception, concealment and blatant lying are major aspects of the illness. This determination to be honest creates a whole new form of safety for me; if it is not secret the illness cannot regain its strength. If I speak it out loud it makes it real, it means I have to acknowledge what I have done and why I must not let it happen.

I have an enormous amount to be thankful for and I am going to fight to hold on to it all. I have a wonderful husband and family of whom I am extremely proud, even though they won't let me run their lives! Sasha is still going extremely strong and is truly beautiful and Monty (our totally loopy Labrador Collie cross), who came as a fixture with Steve, is an absolute joy – even if it did take nearly 2 years for him to accept that I was allowed into the pack! Remarkably, I am finally pursuing a career in acting, what I always dreamed of doing. Even if I don't make it, I was no longer prepared to let the fear stop me. I would much rather try and fail than allow any more of my life to go by without even trying. For years I tried to convince myself that the time had passed and it was too late but, as with many things in life, it is never too late. It is what I need to be doing and it is a huge motivator to stay well, the industry is competitive enough, there is no way I could do myself any kind of justice if I am not in the very best mental, physical and emotional shape I can be.

Something I always have to hold true however, regardless of ambition or anything else is how important it is to never lose sight of what it takes to stay well. Someone very wise, (a recovering alcoholic) told me that my mental health has to take precedence over everything else, all other areas of life could be sorted out later as necessary but every time I struggle with my illness, I must tend to that first. Other things that go wrong in life won't kill me – allowing the illness to take over again could. He is absolutely right except that returning to the depths of the illness *would* kill me, I could not come back from there again.

Even on really black days when it would be so much easier to stop fighting and allow it to just consume me again I have to remember that I have got this far for a reason and I have to find out what that is – to do that I have to stay well, stay safe.

I am slowly beginning to realise that I don't just owe it to the people that love me; I owe it to myself too.

I have anorexia nervosa. I am an anorexic. But that is not all I am.

Chapter 3.   <u>Living With and Moving On</u>

To live through an eating disorder has to be amongst the most testing of experiences for anyone to endure. Not only is the illness incredibly painful, terrifying and dangerous but also add to that the lack of understanding and the stigma attached to mental illness then it is a truly horrific experience. The facts are, however, that people do live with the illness for many, many years and somehow find the strength within them to reach recovery.

Fighting the illness is an incredible uphill struggle and it is different for each person, i.e. some will find certain areas of treatment harder than others. Some of the stories that follow are from people who have made that uphill climb, others are still climbing – all have a story to tell that gives insight and clarity to an illness so misunderstood. I have always said that eating disorders are something that one can't fully understand unless experienced first hand, hopefully through the honesty and bravery of the contributors to this chapter that will be a little less true. There is no story of hope greater than someone who has had their life destroyed but is fighting their way back; it is the wish of all in this chapter that they will help others to believe that there is hope too.

Lorna …

'The biggest revelation is that if I allow myself the freedom to be my own best friend, to relax, to be happy then nothing 'bad' happens. In actual fact, life can be quite fun'

Lorna is proof positive that life in recovery is really possible, she is a wonderful person who is compassionate, determined and brave enough to make the very most of her life in recovery. An excellent example of this strength is that she has even started her own business that is going from strength to strength, a challenge most people without history of serious illness would shy away from. Lorna was, for a long time however, simply not able to allow herself to acknowledge that she had the ability to do anything even close to such an undertaking.

As a child she was very unconfident and was teased by her friends and her brother for being *'a bit podgy'* and this affected her self-esteem from an early age. She always loved animals and wanted to be close to them but was only ever allowed a budgie which, whilst nice creatures, are not the sort of pet to give real comfort or love. As Lorna moved towards her teenage years her body began to change and she *'grew into her weight'*.

She matured physically very quickly and began her periods when she was twelve *'my mum always took pleasure in telling the "shrinks" I saw in later life about how I freaked out when I was told about them'*. Growing up is admittedly difficult for many children but as her body had been the cause of her teasing when younger, the fact that it became developed and had more complicated aspects to it's functioning was rather hard to take.

Throughout her years in junior school Lorna was determined not to stand out, she did not want to be noticed as being clever, (even though she was) she just wanted to be part of the crowd and avoid being teased in any way.

When it was time to take the eleven plus exam, Lorna's low confidence was increased by her Mum making her do extra exercises when none of her friends had to. This emphasised to her how much the exam mattered to her Mum and intensified her own fear of failure. As it turned out Lorna passed with no problems and started at the girls grammar school which she enjoyed, indeed in the first year exams *'I came top of whole year and got the school prize, much to the my disbelief and the disbelief of my parents'*. The fact that her parents were surprised served to heighten Lorna's belief that there must have been some mix up with the papers; it was impossible to conceive that she could really have done so well. The same thing happened the next year but still all Lorna and her parents' felt was disbelief, a very sad fact is that neither party could express pride.

Her wish for the future was to become a vet, *'I only ever said this half-heartedly though, not that I didn't want it, I just got it into my head that I'd never achieve it'*. To the objective observer it would appear that Lorna should have no reason whatsoever to doubt her ability to fulfil this dream and yet she was increasingly only able to think in terms of it being *'too big a task and undertaking'*. The fear of failure became an overwhelming one and by the third year of grammar school *'I was feeling the pressure, the panic and the blind terror that my marks would go down and I would fail – that awful word that said it all!'* Lorna was seeing her worth in terms of exam results and school grades, if she failed with that – she failed as a person *'I started to look around for ways to still be seen as achieving'*.

She began to focus on her weight, thinking that if she could lose any *'puppy fat'* and stop eating biscuits and sweets (i.e. treats) then she would be in control of something. Lorna also became obsessive about her handwriting *'if I could keep perfect books with clear handwriting and not one crossing out then it would compensate for lower marks'*, this was in spite of the fact that no lower marks had been received. The fear of the possibility drove her to *'rewrite my books over and over into the night'* this was in addition to a ritual of exercises. She also began eating less and less, using varied methods to hide the fact from her Mum.

Lorna used to feel anger at being so hungry but *'not being able to eat'* and yet, ironically, these feelings of hunger also made her feel powerful and in control of at least one area of her life. *'I lost weight and felt great'* no one noticed until her Mum was told she was not eating lunch and she was taken to the doctors. *'I felt very depressed, trapped and clammed up'* the panic that Lorna felt resulted in her missing school and not speaking for about six weeks.

As she was not too thin at that time the doctor diagnosed *'teenage depression'* and she was prescribed *'happy pills'*. The pills may have worked to a certain extent as she was able to return to school and started to speak again but the rewriting of books and dodging food increased and she got more and more deceitful about managing it all. It got to the point where the weight loss was very noticeable and she was taken to the doctors again, *'a psychiatrist then came to the house, he asked me if I ate potatoes or bread – when I said not much he diagnosed anorexia!'*

After that she was taken into hospital and given a target weight to reach on the basis of reward and punishment treatment *'I wanted out, I was scared to death in there'*. Lorna was kept on a high dose of a sedative throughout this treatment; she recalls that this drug was called largactil although she readily admits that it is hard to remember. What she can recall is how that drug made her feel *'this "largactil" made my legs feel like lead, I felt stupefied and unable to move'*.

And yet her mind remained active with the *'fear of having to put on weight and the general depression of my situation'*. It is rather hard to understand the benefit of such a drug. In an attempt to reach target quicker she ate big bars of chocolate sandwiched between thick bread and butter *'to this day, chocolate is not in the least appealing to me.'* The psychiatric counselling in hospital involved Lorna being told that she was afraid of sex and boys, *'I was only just 14 and hadn't given either a thought'*, she was only obsessed with the neatness of her books.

By this stage the obsessive behaviour had increased, *'I could not make a mark on paper without wanting to erase it, destroy it – it just wasn't good enough'* Lorna felt too scared to tell anyone this and as soon as she was released she lost the weight again. So began several years of weight yo-yoing and spells of hospitalisation, she missed so much school that at 16 she left, without the qualifications she was capable of. Lorna became more and more isolated as she didn't feel able to spend time with any friends *'I found it painful to be with them, as if I was behind a brick wall that I couldn't get over to reach them'*.

One of the spells in hospital lasted a year (going home at weekends), she felt that she didn't want to be at home but *'I just didn't know where I wanted to be'*. Very disturbingly at one point during her time in hospital she discovered that she had been given lithium, she doesn't even know why. It came to light after she told the hospital staff she was having dizzy spells, it turned out this drug *'should be signed for consent to take it and blood tests to monitor it – this wasn't done!'*

Both in and out of hospital she was on temazepam (sleeping tablets) and *'until it was frowned upon to give them out willy-nilly'* she was on valium too. When at home these had to be hidden from her as she would get *'frantic for valium and on really black days I'd take the lot'*, on one such occasion Lorna took the whole bottle of sleeping pills which led to a stomach pump and another hospital admission.

What Lorna has been through in hospital is so disturbing, in addition to the 'treatments' mentioned previously she even endured two courses of electro convulsive therapy (electric shock treatment to the brain), this started when she was 18. Lorna was approached to sign for it when she was alone in hospital and she refused (understandably) saying that she wanted to speak to her Mum, this she was told, was *'another sign that I was "trying to stay a child"'*. Lorna signed and her Mum didn't seem to be against it, *'I was scared but desperate to try anything to help me forget my situation'*. E.C.T basically consists of *'an injection of anaesthetic that lasts for a few minutes, everyone then sat in a queue and waited. I was the only person under (about) 50 in the room'*. When it was Lorna's turn she had to lie on a bed and have another injection, when a gum shield had been inserted *'the convulsion is then sent through with two electrodes on the side of your head'*. As bizarre as it may sound, Lorna actually felt jealous of the other women going through treatment *'they'd come round and not know what day it was or where the heck they were! I longed for this oblivion and was annoyed when I came round that I knew that I was still me'*.

Considering what she was having to endure, such feelings are understandable especially as the E.C.T had no positive effect at all. This E.C.T was followed by various courses of different anti-depressants again it is difficult for Lorna to recall the names, although Amitriptyline is one she remembers. She reached the point that many sufferers do, when she didn't care *'what I was taking I just wanted to feel different, part of the world and not scared to be'*.

The next few years were wasted, being in and out of hospital *'doing crazy things like running away from hospital in pyjamas!'* Lorna was just not thinking clearly though and always ran home to her Mums, the last place she really wanted to be *'I felt dominated and controlled by Mum'*. On one night in particular after one of the escape acts she was put on the 'lock up' ward for the night, as this was general psychiatry and it was where the most serious cases stayed *'I lay all night listening to the goings on'*, not an experience easily forgotten.

As the behaviours increased it got to the point where she was recommended for a brain operation, she was told that she was an 'intractable' case and was led to believe that *'my only way to recovery and escaping depression was this brain operation'*. It was to be a lobotomy or leucotomy (she cannot recall which it was) and it was explained to her that they would cut the connection between the two halves of her brain. This could be performed through her nostrils so there would be no cutting or scarring, she was also told that there would be some months of recuperation where she would have to learn such things as holding a knife and fork again. In Lorna's ill state she thought this sounded like *'an escape from knowing who I was and being me'* she agreed to the operation. When things progressed however, the brain surgeon told her that she should never have been recommended for it and it wouldn't help, would make no difference to her at all. These events show clearly how little the professionals dealing with Lorna knew about eating disorders and how to treat them.

For the year that followed Lorna was on anti-depressants, mainly Prozac, and at bad times on sedatives also. The brain operation that never happened was actually 'a catalyst for a sudden pendulum swing in my illness'. Lorna was almost forced to realise how sick she was of her life, how trapped she felt and how she always 'thought about life as this frightening "baddie" that I didn't know how to handle'.

In many ways she wanted to be with her mum as a child and this seemed to be exactly what her mum wanted 'Mum was, I felt, almost disappointed about the brain operation not being done,' as her Mum was unhappy with her own life, Lorna was her main focus, to relive Lorna's childhood again would have given that focus new strength. For Lorna, there was also a pull towards a new urge to 'break out and almost be outrageous'. It was true to say that after years of being dictated by her illness and being in and out of hospital with numerous failed treatments Lorna really did not know what she wanted.

At this point her illness began to manifest itself very differently, without even knowing why she began to eat and eat. She would lock herself away in her room with the curtains shut, a book and a pile of food, the rest of the time she slept to 'shut the world out'. Lorna still feels ashamed of what she ate 'I felt so disgusting, so totally and utterly disgusting, disgusting, disgusting and so totally and utterly out of control'.

Sleep and books became her escapism, 'novels telling stories of people whose life I wished I lived – wished I had the courage to live' she felt such a deep loathing for her growing fat but simply couldn't stop 'it was total mental rebellion'. After a few weeks of this regime she began using other behaviours to try and lose the weight again, in fact the hospital actually wanted to admit her to lose the weight!

The irony of it was almost too much to believe but for once she felt that she actually had some power, as her increased weight was not a physical threat to her she was able to say that there was *'no way'* she was going back in to hospital. From some deep recess in her mind Lorna was beginning to feel something different *'it had been squashed and hidden for so long but I wanted to take back control of my life, to actually do something with it'*. This was the first time for a long time that she had felt anything really positive and she tried to act on it *'I even attempted to go back to college'* this was made so difficult by the fact that she was still terrified of people her own age as she still felt so removed from them and couldn't think about life the way they did.

Lorna genuinely believed that when enrolling to redo her 'O' levels she would be able to cope with the handwriting and neatness obsession, she couldn't *'I was still totally phobic about my handwriting and leaving any mark on the paper'*. On the first day of college as her mother saw her off she started to cry, when Lorna asked her why she was crying she said that she was happy that Lorna was getting a life. Lorna felt that it was more because she was losing her to her life; this made Lorna angry and determined to make a success of college.

On the first day however she tried to write her timetable and from that moment the rewriting everything started again, all her positive and good intentions were still being masked by aspects of the illness *'nothing I did was ever good enough'*. This time Lorna actually felt worse as she *'couldn't even console and protect myself with the knowledge that I was the thinnest girl in the class'* this knowledge intensified all the negative things she had ever thought about herself. *'I had felt ugly for as long as I could remember, but now I felt enormously, hideously, disgustingly fat and uglier than ever, ever before'* it was at this point that even more damaging behaviours began to take hold.

Lorna devised for herself a ritualised process where she was always going to wipe the slate clean and everything would be ok. This meant that if *'I had eaten something I shouldn't have done or I wanted to change the way I had written some work, or I thought I'd done or said*

something wrong then I would punish myself' these 'punishments' took the form of bingeing and purging and, of course, owing to the nature of the illness there were far more causes to punish than there were days that ended without Lorna hurting herself. Perversely though the punishments were more a comfort than anything else, they provided a release from trying to be a *'new person'* who lived the same way, or at least tried to live the same way, as other people of the same age.

It was as though she was simply not able to function normally, for so long she had existed governed by the illness that *'I found it curiously difficult to be 'normal' without an 'abnormal' problem'*. Although Lorna partly felt that she wanted to move into the 'normal' life completely, the other part of her was still so dominant and told her that she did not deserve to be normal. With hindsight she believes that more than being undeserving it was actually the fact that she did not believe she could achieve it, once again the fear of failure gave the illness all the fuel it needed. In a way, Lorna believes that this thinking led her to *'set out to fail'* she continually functioned on the cycle of thinking that she had done things wrongly. This belief along with still feeling so *'cut off'* from those around her kept sending her back to *'the old friend – food and the abuse of it'*.

The irony is that at this time, she did have friends although it was very hard for her to accept this *'it was a revelation to me that I developed friendships where girls wanted to see me out of college - just for company!'* It was hard for Lorna to see any worth in herself and so found it difficult to believe that others could see anything either, however, she tried really hard to do the 'normal' things in life and even felt able to confide in a friend about her illness. By this time Lorna feels that at least part of her was trying to accept that *'I couldn't fight and hide from normality and life – it presented itself against my will'.*

As her periods started again she had the added challenge of allowing herself to accept the changes to her body. She found this easier to cope with my talking to her sister about it rather than to her mum, she felt that her mum would try to *'take over my periods again'*, meaning that her mother would attempt to control how she dealt with this big change. It was around this time that she had her 21st birthday and she even asked if she could have a big party *'I asked as many people as I could think of, I desperately wanted to fill the room with people that were there because they might like me'* it is sad to say that although a lot of people did come, Lorna was only able to count those that didn't.

Even though she was desperately trying to move into a 'normal' social life, Lorna was simply unable to shake off the overwhelming negative train of thought that prevented her from feeling good about any aspect of it. At the time of her 21st she was on yet another diet and she hated herself for the fact that she felt hungry *'I had lost self control and this felt disgusting'* of course these feelings gave her illness the excuse to resume the punishment regime. Every time she hurt herself she swore it would be the last time, it didn't stop this easily however and despite attending therapy and counselling nothing improved *'it never got to the core of my thinking and being – I didn't let it'.*

Lorna's illness constantly guarded her from having to face up to the reality of how she felt, her fear of failure and fear of the unknown were so great that she had to hide from them *'I was playing at trying and at this stage had no intention of letting go'.* Indeed, the thoughts, feelings and consequent behaviours were so deeply entrenched that letting go would have exposed her to a life she had no experience of dealing with in a 'normal' way, she genuinely felt that *'I was an "eating disorder"'*. This is a facet of the illness that those who have not experienced it could find very hard to understand, the illness robs sufferers of themselves – they lose sight of who they really are.

Sadly college fell by the wayside, a victim of the handwriting obsession and punishment regime with continual assertions that tomorrow she'd start afresh. Lorna spent most of her time at home with her parents and beloved dog, Ben. Her mum was then diagnosed with bowel cancer and after several operations Lorna became her carer and took over the running of the house for her dad and brother. After only a short time the cancer was diagnosed as terminal *'I felt very scared and coped by thinking that maybe I'd kill myself when she died'*, the family went on holiday to Jersey and both Lorna and her mother resented the fact that her father was there. *'I thought I hated him so much'*.

Of course, it is far more likely that this assumed hatred for her father was really conjured up to focus her feelings on because it was so much easier than facing the emotions associated with her mother's illness. Whilst in Jersey her mum had to go into hospital and they had to stay on until she stabilised, during this time Lorna lost her virginity to a hotel waiter *'I thought I may as well before I killed myself'*. It was a revelation to her that someone would find her attractive and on that night she decided that she would at least try to go on living after her mum's death. In spite of this decision, she still punished herself for what she had done, convincing her that it was wrong and she deserved to hurt. Her mum died soon after this.

Throughout this period, Lorna was not receiving any professional intervention at all, the illness was just accepted as part of her life that was such a compulsion that there seemed no reason to try and work for recovery.

It did move to the point, however, where Lorna was able to function with the illness in tow; at 24 she got her first job and soon after moved to Jersey to live and work. It was a half-baked intention that moving to Jersey would give her the opportunity of a fresh start, free from the behaviours and self-hatred that governed so much of her existence. *'Unfortunately my inner self had done it's own packing'* and after just a few days in Jersey she found herself back in exactly the same pattern of obsession, self hatred, and rituals.

She had the very best of intentions but was possibly misjudging the strength of the illness *'my brain unpacked too and all the habits and rituals were still there, not a crease from transit'* she tried to stop the behaviours when she had settled there but again to no avail.

Lorna began to employ yet more *'coping mechanisms'* for example she discovered *'clubs, dancing and alcohol'* – she also discovered that men liked her, something she had previously believed to be impossible. After receiving a marriage proposal Lorna returned home to live with her sister in a total panic about her life, she felt that returning to a safer environment might help to make sense of things.

A job in a local hotel unfortunately only served to make her feel worse about herself as she felt that she wasn't able to do anything really successfully. The behaviours intensified *'life was a round of the old punishment rituals and going out to a local nightclub where I would 'pick up' any man I singled out'*. Lorna used this process as a gauge as to whether she likeable and an acceptable person, if she was *'successful'* with a man then she was – if not she was worthless. The irony of this was that she would still go and punish herself afterwards either way. She still feels ashamed of behaving this way especially as she was aware that *'I never really loved anyone'*, although she is able to acknowledge that this was largely due to *'not being capable of loving as I didn't love myself'* she was trying to achieve this through them liking her, without success.

Unfortunately things were about to become even harder, her sister Judith, with whom she was very close, was diagnosed with terminal cancer and Lorna could only cope through her illness, something of which she is ashamed. *'I tried to be a support to Judith but I must have been a frustration and a worry too'* it was again a struggle trying to be the person she wanted to be whilst battling the ill part of her. Lorna experienced further guilt and shame that *'whilst Judith could not control what was happening to her body, I was abusing mine'* but she felt powerless to stop it.

These feelings were heightened when, just a month before Judith died, Lorna found her father dead in his home – he had suffered a heart attack. It was almost too much to bear, the knowledge that all her family (apart from her brother) had died. However, it did somehow give her new determination to live but she felt that she needed a focus, something to care for; she needed to feel needed – to have a purpose.

It was around this time that she began to take in stray cats that needed treatment and a home, she became such a regular visitor at the vets that she was offered the chance to train on the job as a receptionist/veterinary nurse. It was a chance that Lorna took and it worked out better than she could have imagined for it was there that she met Dave – a locum vet at the surgery. *'He was and still is a wonderful support'* Lorna was able to tell him about the eating problems she still had and although she has *'driven him to distraction'* he continually tried to help. *'I nearly destroyed our relationship with my problem'* it was just impossible for Lorna to accept that he actually loved her for the person she really was/is, *'I was so scared it would end that I nearly pushed him into it'*.

Lorna felt as though the relationship was a triangle between herself, Dave and *'the other part of me'* although she was feeling part of a couple and proud to be so, she just couldn't let go of the part that seemed compelled to destroy everything. *'I was beginning to have feelings I'd never had*

87

for anyone before' and yet that happiness was clouded by the fear that she was not able to truly define what was going on and felt that *'if one couldn't define happiness, then one might lose it'*. This belief could be explained by Lorna's constant fear of failure, if she could not define something then she could not control it and if it could not be controlled then she would not be able to hold on to it – she would fail.

In a desperate effort to beat it Lorna began attending therapy once more and Dave attended some sessions too, she began to let go of the behaviours and thought she was better. It was a long road though and for a while she slipped back into the anorexia *'my desire to be back in control led me once again into over control'* and this led to a passionate argument with Dave *'I was not very good, in fact was totally incapable of being 'nice' to myself'*. It is very hard for someone who loves a sufferer of anorexia to understand how he or she can hurt themselves, hate themselves so much. *'It took time to get the hang of it, but gradually, Dave taught me how to really value who I am, what I am and say those three words 'I deserve it''* Lorna firmly believes that she would not have survived one period of 'punishment' which left her with severe heart palpitations that felt as though her heart would stop at any minute.

It was probably the turning point for Lorna as she saw more plainly than ever before that if she did not fight it, she could lose everything to this horrendous illness. *'Then I started, with Dave's help, to build a normal life that I had always believed I could not achieve'* it was so hard for her to accept that she could make it and she had to face many extremely difficult changes in thought processes. *'The hardest lesson to learn was to be my own best friend, learning to think that I am allowed to be relaxed, happy (even decadent sometimes) and like myself'*.

These may seem strange things to have to learn but after years of negative conditioning it is essential to relearn in order to recover. Negative thoughts in the anorexic mind become a safe way to exist and to attempt to alter that status, and cope with the change takes a lot of time and will.

Reaching life in recovery is not easy, especially when the illness has had the controlling influence for so long *'I won't say that it is all a bed of roses, but then who's life is?'* accepting that it is normal to have a bad day is also an integral part of getting well.

Even now, Lorna still takes the anti-depressant Cipramil but she does not see this a failure, she simply recognises that *'Dave and I have a very stressful life with the business and I haven't yet learnt all the best coping mechanisms to handle it'* she firmly believes that these will come with time. Through therapy, the support of some one close and truly wanting it, Lorna knows that recovery is a process that will happen.

Aspects of the illness will hang around even when well into recovery but increasingly these will be thoughts rather than actual damaging behaviours *'I will often say "Do I look fat?" Or I will look at my stomach believing it sticks out or will scowl at myself in the mirror because I think I look ugly'*. Lorna is now more able than she has ever been to recognise these thoughts for what they really are and is able to deal with them in 'healthy' ways, she also knows how miserable her self loathing can make those who love her, and so she is better positioned than ever to keep fighting it.

Lorna is so much into life in recovery that she is able to express positive feelings about her life and her future, something that she would never have dared to do before through the fear of failure or the belief of her being unworthy of anything positive.

The years of emotional and physical pain could have destroyed her totally and yet somehow she has found the strength to not only start the fight but to keep it going against the part of herself that damaged her, and her life for so long.

'Now I want to live my life, not destroy it'.

Jo ...

'No-one had even mentioned to me about my weight or condition, I think people were too scared to, and it's easy to see why.'

Jo is 26 years old and has lived with anorexia since the age of 14, at least it was around this time that she realised that things weren't right, although it only really *'took hold'* when she was 17. Despite the length of her illness she has only recently come into contact with any professional treatment services, indeed *'the first intervention of any kind I received wasn't until 1998, when I was 23'.*

Jo is an extremely talented artist, is intelligent and beautiful and should be enjoying all the pleasures of life and yet she has been trapped in this illness, for a long time without help or even acknowledgement. She is very quick to acknowledge how difficult the illness is to understand, even when you are living it *'I myself didn't really know what was happening, I suppose I did in some ways since I was aware that I was caught in this trap, aware of what I was doing but I didn't really understand why'.* The fact that the illness can take over without the person having the opportunity to make sense of it or to halt its progression is a terrifying aspect of the illness of which few people are aware. *'I had no understanding of anorexia at all'* sufferers are not able to understand the illness when it takes hold any more than the observer can.

It is only as time passes and the person eventually receives the right sort of treatment can any sense be made of what is really going on *'it's only in the past two years, through inpatient care, that I have come to understand the illness more'.* It is often very true that it is only through treatment, really concentrated care, can any level of understanding be reached but it is sadly also true that it often takes far too long to receive such treatment *'I wish this help had come sooner'*.

Jo is, unfortunately, able to give a clear example of how the illness is one of those things that people just do not want to see. Humans are adept at ignoring that which scares them, that which they cannot understand. In the case of illnesses such as eating disorders this denial on the part of those around the sufferer can actually be very damaging. Although people cannot be blamed for this, as they can't know that their actions (or lack of action) are making matters worse, it is true to say that, as with most things in life, the ostrich approach (i.e. head in the sand) rarely has any result other than a negative one. *'The fact that no-one ever mentioned my increasingly low weight just reconfirmed my fears of myself to me, and so I continued as if nothing was wrong'*, at the time Jo understandably believed that if she had looked thin people would have said something. This, of course, was partly the illness causing her to think this way – i.e. if there was no reason to stop, carry on!

Aside from the illness, very ordinary thinking would have led her to the same conclusion; if one does not receive concern (or even criticism) then what reason it there to change anything. As unbelievable as it may seem, Jo was actually working as a waitress whilst weighing only 5 stone – not even her boss said anything (but how many people would be able to?)! Jo believes that fear of her reaction was a factor involved in why no-one approached her about her weight *'I don't know how I would have reacted if he (her boss) did, and maybe he was too afraid of this'*. Even those closest to the sufferer often don't know what to say, or are too afraid of the reaction *'I know now that this is why my family would not broach the subject with me – they felt helpless'*.

The lack of understanding that surrounds eating disorders can put up a very definite barrier between the sufferer and those around them; they become almost shrouded by something that is a total mystery. The nature of the illness is also such that the person will go to great lengths to conceal it, the obvious physical symptoms cannot be concealed forever but the behaviours can. *'I feel that the secret nature and lack of knowledge is why anorexia often goes untreated'* indeed, it is true to say that many sufferers have been ill for a long time before they receive an accurate diagnosis and, consequently treatment. This is not least because, for a variety of reasons, the illness compels the person to protect the secret at all costs – even though this often means lying to those closest to them.

'When people finally do ask you if something is wrong, you deny it, even when inside you are screaming out for help' this is a protection mechanism on the part of the illness and is one of the most destructive aspects of anorexic thinking. It was when Jo actually collapsed that there could be no further denial, from Jo herself or those close to her, that something was seriously wrong – she was taken to a doctor. This, again creates very mixed emotions from the person, the part which has been crying out is finally being heard and yet the ill part is desperate to cling to that which has become so familiar *'I've never felt so relieved, yet so frightened as I did at that point'.* Jo partly attributes this intense fear to the stories she had heard about the treatment of anorexics in hospital, none of these had been positive and the prospect of what lay ahead was terrifying *'I'd only heard stories of people going into hospital where they were force-fed; not allowed to see friends and relatives; their clothes being taken until they gained weight etc.'* Naturally this was a frightening thing to face and as Jo describes the illness as *'the 'security' I had found for myself',* it is little wonder that although she desperately wanted to be helped, facing the unknown felt absolutely awful.

It is important to note at this point that Jo had already been ill for around nine years, this intervention was a sign that she would be losing the way of life that had become deeply entrenched – all consuming in fact and all of a sudden that was to be challenged in appalling ways, so she thought. However, Jo considers herself very lucky in that the horror stories she had heard did not happen, in fact just the opposite was true *'my G.P was very persistent and found me a place in one of the best specialist units in the country'*.

Although the treatment was very different to that which she had heard about, Jo recognises (with the benefit of hindsight) that it was simply *'too much too soon'*. One day she was admitted, the next she was told that she would be there until she reached the target weight set for her of 9 stone 5 pounds. Whilst it was the case that people of Jo's height and build who do not have the illness will most likely weigh something around that amount, for Jo this concept was very frightening *'I'd never been this weight, even before I was ill'*. To expect a person to, not only gain weight, but reach a weight that is totally alien to them is asking a great deal of anyone. This is particularly true of an anorexic who has existed at a very low weight for a long time, the physical change and the emotions that evokes is simply too great for a person to deal with. *'I can see that this 'target weight' style of treatment is extremely successful, but only when the patient has chosen it for themselves, and is ready for it'*.

Jo is adamant that being ready is of paramount importance; a target weight should be set through consultation not just when *'family and doctors are just desperate to do something before it is too late'*. In spite of this, seemingly impossible, target weight Jo sees this period in hospital as being *'extremely useful'*. Not only did her weight increase, i.e. became physically more safe but *'it gave me an insight and understanding of what was happening to me'* this was not least because, through being in a safe and controlled environment she was given time to really think and consider where she was within herself. During this time there was also the startling realisation that *'people actually understood how I was feeling, and how openly patients could talk to people'*, having endured the illness alone for so many years without being challenged over it at all it was extraordinary to find that *'for the first time, I saw that I wasn't the only person going through it'.*

Unfortunately, in spite of the positive things about the admission, Jo admits that she was *'eating my way out'.* Due to her low weight, as is the case with many sufferers, she was simply not able to cope with the intense therapy and in the end was set what is termed a safe weight at which she would be allowed to leave. *'I reached 45kg on the Wednesday, and I was home by the Friday'* this was simply too quick and it was at this point that Jo feels she was let down *'I had no follow up treatment, so ultimately, within a month I had lost 10 kilos and was desperate to be in hospital'.*

The feeling of being supported and then totally abandoned is an incredibly hard thing to deal with – especially when suffering from an illness that causes the person to deal with things through avoidance behaviours. The illness 'copes' with life through the use of these behaviours but it relies on secrecy to do so *'I was so unhappy, as now everyone was aware of my condition. My secret world had been taken away and I wanted help'.* Exposing the illness makes the person so vulnerable, this is the point where the need for help becomes imperative – although the person is still in the grip of the illness, the fear of what is to come is terrifying – to face that alone is truly dreadful.

The next stage was to try and work on the issues of which she was now aware, but through the feelings she experienced on being discharged from hospital Jo knew that she needed help to do that. The hospital agreed to admit her on the target weight programme; this was mainly due to the fact that, as it was *'me wanting to do it, and choosing it for myself'* i.e. the chances of real progress were greater. Unfortunately, with hindsight, she can now see that this was still much too soon. Although Jo reached the target weight set for her, her illness caused her to battle against the treatment the whole way through *'this left me at a normal weight but with all my anorexic thoughts and attitudes still there'.*

Due to the illness still having so much strength, she simply could not maintain a steady weight and was eventually discharged – a condition of treatment was that patients maintain the target weight they are set. Despite knowing that the treatment was not progressing, Jo was desperate to stay in hospital *'but only because it seemed 'safe' I think'*. The illness can provide a feeling of 'safety' for sufferers because it seems so familiar and (at least in the early stages) it makes it possible to bear life. When the illness does not belong in the secret life of the sufferer anymore, the world becomes terrifying again and safety is sought.

As a consequence of being discharged from this assumed safety Jo was once again left to cope with things largely alone and this was an impossible situation to be in. *'I lost all the weight I had gained as soon as I returned home, it had been so long since I had eaten normally, I'd simply lost all concept of what a person needs to eat'* whilst a hospital environment may appear safe, to be discharged back to the old environment with very little support is almost worse than never having been in hospital.

Even through a limited time in treatment, all kinds of issues and consequent thoughts and feelings are brought to the surface. If these are then not dealt with in the safe, confined environment of a treatment unit, they can seriously intensify the symptoms and cause increased difficulties for the person.

This is the point at which Jo sees the most significant gap in the services available for the treatment of eating disorders, the difference between inpatient and outpatient treatment is massive. The patient goes from hospital staff having total control of everything they eat, drink and do with the necessary support, to having often nothing more than a weekly one-hour session. This is a huge difference and an extremely difficult time for someone who has reached recovery, let alone someone who is still (at least partially) in the grip of the illness.

However, Jo is also well aware of the painful truth that *'whatever treatment is available, even the best, will not work unless the patient themselves wants it and is ready for recovery'* and this has been one of the main barriers preventing Jo from reaching recovery. It is an extremely awkward situation as the illness creates such a powerful barrier *'this is extremely difficult as even when you know you want to recover and are desperate for a way out, the pull of the illness is so strong'*; it can even feel as though the person is somehow betraying himself or herself in wanting to recover.

This sense of betrayal then leads to an overwhelming sense of guilt, intensifying the guilt the sufferer may feel about other things, this guilt is about daring *'to feel that you are worth more than this life'*. In some ways this could be described as having two voices *'an objective rational one and an 'anorexic' one'*, the person finds himself or herself in what Jo calls a *'constant battle'*.

This is why Jo feels that a lot more support is needed for people who are living in the community with their illness, and after inpatient care. *'Continual re-feeding in hospital and then discharge, only to return home to the same situation is no solution'* this is a situation of which Jo has had bitter experience and is firmly of the belief that *'more therapy based outpatient services are desperately required'*. Owing to Jo's own experience of the consequence of delay in recognition and diagnosis she believes that the *'best treatment of all'* is to catch the illness as soon as possible, the sooner it is diagnosed the better the chance of recovery. As the illness becomes an all consuming way of life, controlling thought, feelings and actions it is the case that the longer one lives with it the more it becomes a way of life and so much harder and more terrifying to fight against.

A further aspect, which Jo considers to be of great importance, is that more should be done in schools to make people aware of the condition. Such awareness could increase the number of people who receive help early and would help to reduce the number of young people developing anorexia. *'Children need to learn to accept themselves and their individuality and I think this could begin in the classroom'*, it is also important that children are made aware of the importance of expressing emotions and dealing with them in 'healthy' ways. *'Making teachers and people in general, more aware of the condition could mean early intervention and therefore diagnosis if anorexia did occur'.*

A *'huge problem'* regarding actual treatment, in Jo's experience, is the difference that where a person lives can make to the treatment received. There is no option but to use the services available in ones own area and these vary immensely, due partly to the general lack of good treatment facilities overall. Jo raises the point that with the *'growing awareness, and also growing occurrence, of this illness, should have resulted in a huge expanse of treatment facilities for this condition by now'*. She is quick to note, however that she feels sure that anyone suffering from any illness would feel the same way about the treatment of their condition – sadly it is in part the case that *'this all comes down to money'.*

It is sad to say that often decisions made by local health authorities regarding what treatment a person will receive is based on whether they have funding available/a contract in place with a good treatment service which still has the funding left for another patient (see chapter 5). Again this is sadly another aspect of which Jo has had very difficult experience, those that control the money and make the decisions often have very little understanding of the nature of the illness and consequently place all sorts of conditions on patients e.g. if they can maintain their weight until a certain date, then they can have inpatient treatment!

Another difficulty Jo notes with regards to treatment is the fact that it can manifest itself in so many different ways, the triggers for the illness vary greatly for one person to another and the behaviours involved are vastly varied too. *'This can make diagnosis, and ultimately treatment, very difficult'.* Jo feels without doubt that the most important factor in any form of treatment is *'the readiness and co-operation of the patient'* it is simply not possible to treat a person with an eating disorder if they are not in the necessary position to receive that treatment. *'They need to be willing and really wanting treatment, they need to receive empathy not sympathy, firmness but not strict force-feeding or reward and punishment systems and most importantly, understanding'.*

Being able to see that people are around wanting to help and feeling able to trust those people enough to begin to open up to them is so incredibly important, not all treatments allow this to happen. Jo further considers that there is no substitute for time *'this is such a complex illness that recovery is ultimately a long and slow road – but worth it'* an awareness of this for the sufferer themselves and for all those around them is imperative to reach life in recovery.

The person must never be allowed to lose sight of all the possibilities they will have beyond the illness, no matter how long it may take they will get there and their future will be very different to their existence with the illness. Jo is very much aware of what is needed to reach recovery (and what does not work) and is determined to keep fighting until she gets there.

'I am still on this road (to recovery) but I firmly believe that it is possible to escape the grip of anorexia'.

Steve …

'I hope there will be an end to this, I have had enough now. Nobody, not anyone deserves to suffer like this.'

It is incredibly hard for anyone to cope with living with an eating disorder, but for a man it is in some ways far worse. At the very least it is somehow acceptable for a woman to have the illness but for a man, surely it's a *'woman's thing'*? The sad fact is that many men do experience some form of the illness, despite the fact that it is predominately female (see chapter 1) and they often have to endure the effects of the associated stigma more than women do and are even more open to misdiagnosis and lack of understanding.

Steve is caring and very sensitive with so much to offer and yet, since school, he has been prevented from truly living his life due to the destructive effects of anorexia. Although still in the grip of the illness, Steve is holding on to the belief that anorexia can be beaten and that he will recover.

He remembers the first time he really became aware of his weight very vividly, he was 11 and due to start secondary school. Everyone had new blazers with the school emblem on them, the problem was that his Mum could not find one big enough and so bought a plain one and sewed the emblem on the blazer herself. Being different amongst 500 boys was not the kind of start to a new school that anyone would want and for Steve it was almost unbearable *'how did I feel? Embarrassed wouldn't be the word, I wanted to lose weight straight away'*. The teasing that was to last throughout Steve's school life began and he was desperate to lose the weight, understandably he believed that if he could remove the main thing about himself that was obviously different perhaps the attention would stop.

His distress was not really acknowledged at home however *'Mum insisted that I eat a cooked breakfast before going to school, she said if I didn't eat it she would call the Headmaster and tell him'*. Steve was terrified of any disapproval and the thought of the Headmaster being contacted was dreadful as he believed it would only serve to make the situation at school even worse. He hated school and could not wait to leave as soon as he possibly could, the school environment and all the pressure and teasing that went with it were something that Steve knew he needed to escape from. *'I decided to lose weight as soon as I left school, I would be my own boss from now on. Nobody was going to tell me what to eat'* the decision to lose weight was not just to remove the thing that caused the teasing but also to gain some sense of control in a life that had for years been a difficult struggle.

After leaving school at 16, Steve got a job on a farm and as he loved animals and the countryside, he felt really happy there and for a while, gained a lot of weight. This was not to last however as suddenly he wanted rid of this excess weight and set himself a fixed eating regime that did not vary for 6 months. During this time he lost a large amount of weight and began a strict exercise regime, people began to notice *'they said I looked terrible, so thin, they said I looked like a walking skeleton'* it was a bizarre thing for Steve to hear as he just wanted to lose some excess weight.

The first time he heard the word anorexia was from one such concerned person, this meant nothing to Steve *'... said I'd got anorexia, what? I'd never even heard of it'* it was only when he realised how worried his mum was that he tried to stop the strict regime.

Soon after this he met the love of his life and they bought a house together, this marked a much happier time. However, although he managed to eat breakfast and an evening meal, food and weight were always on his mind. In spite of this, life was pretty good for a while, Steve left the farm and began lorry driving, he and his wife had a comfortable routine and everything seemed fine. Steve was, for many years, able to control the nagging negative thoughts that played on his mind – that was until one day about 4 years ago. Totally without warning his wife said that she was leaving, no explanation and the very next day she was gone *'we were together for 14 years, 12 of those* married and it was such a terrible shock. I never felt pain so bad'.

After this Steve suffered a nervous breakdown, was put on anti-depressants and referred to a clinical psychology department. He stopped eating the day Jane left and didn't eat for 5 months (survived by drinking hot chocolate), his G.P would not believe this however (hence the psychiatric referral); 'he made me out to be lying to him, made me feel so small'. Steve recognises that to survive for that length of time without proper food may seem impossible, but in the world of an anorexic the body copes with an incredible amount.

Obviously there are severe health implications in trying to exist without food but the fact that the doctor totally dismissed even the possibility was Steve's first indication that his condition would not be correctly diagnosed. Steve firmly believes that this was because he is male. During his visits to this clinic he saw 10 different doctors; ironically the first was the best! 'He realised how thin I was and weighed me and took a blood sample, he prescribed Fortisips (calorie, vitamin drinks) to try and make up for the calories and vitamins I was missing' although prescribed 8 a day, Steve could only drink 3 for fear of gaining weight. Again this shows the total lack of understanding of Steve's condition, to give an anorexic well in the grip of the illness a weight gain drink to go away and consume without help or support of any kind is simply not going to work.

After a month Steve returned for a follow up appointment and his weight had dropped to a dangerous level and the doctor wanted to hospitalise him straight away. The blood tests had shown internal damage to his liver and kidneys and so his body was becoming increasingly fragile. The problem was that 'he (the doctor) wanted me to sign a form to say that I was voluntarily going into hospital and I would agree to eat' at this point Steve had not received counselling or therapy of any kind and was deep into the illness, and yet this doctor was expecting that he could start eating again with no trouble at all. To make matters even worse, he had no alternative to offer Steve and was totally baffled by Steve's apparent wish to starve himself to death *'when I said I couldn't sign the form, he seemed lost for words. He then just made me another appointment for a month's time'.* It may be concluded that if a doctor has deemed that a patient is in need of hospitalisation, and then goes to the other end of the scale and does not see that person again for a month, then there is clearly little understanding of the seriousness of the illness.

When Steve returned for his next appointment that doctor had left and his replacement told him that if she could sort out his depression then his appetite would return, no question of there being an illness causing his weight loss just that he simply was not eating because he did not feel like it! The next monthly appointment saw yet another change of doctor and this process continued for a year, every appointment there was a different doctor. Each doctor Steve saw prescribed a different sort of anti-depressant, increasing in strength each time until it reached the point where they made him so drowsy he was not able to work.

Still there was no mention of treatment for the anorexia; the focus was purely on depression and even that just revolved around prescription of medication – no counselling or therapy whatsoever, no attempt to establish what was really going on at all. It is interesting to consider whether this would have been the case if he were female, probably not.

Things looked a little more promising when he was finally referred to a clinical psychologist who actually talked to him about how he was feeling. *'Talking with her seemed to help a bit; we talked about my feelings after my break up with Jane. She said that the eating disorder and the depression were linked'* this was the first time that Steve had experienced a professional recognising what was wrong. Although Steve found talking about his problems extremely difficult, it did help him to recognise that he had a problem with food long before he met Jane.

The psychologist wanted him to attend an eating disorders clinic, which had a meeting every week with other sufferers and doctors. The problem was that she warned him he would almost certainly be the only male there, *'I just felt too embarrassed to attend, I couldn't face walking into a room on my own like that'.*

When self-confidence is at such low ebb it is extremely difficult to do anything, especially when it is something that must be done alone and as a minority figure. The next appointment was to meet with a dietician and only lasted about 10 minutes; he was given a diet sheet and told what he should be eating. Steve tried to explain that he could not eat what the dietician was recommending, *'at the time I wasn't eating at all and she wanted me to eat 3 meals a day!'* On hearing this, the dietician simply said that she could not do anything for him; he just got up and left.

The feeling of desperation was overwhelming *'I felt so low; I went home and was as close as I've ever been to ending it all. I had all the pills in my hand ready to swallow but thought of my mum and I couldn't do that to her'*, it was impossible to bear the prospect of living with the illness any longer but he simply could not cause his mum that pain.

After falling so low Steve did not feel able to go back to the clinic and has not been for the past 18 months. He felt that it did not do any good being pushed from one doctor to another and prescribed different medication that only made him feel worse. Even when seeing a psychologist who did make a correct diagnosis no one was able to help, or at least Steve felt that they could not. Being a male with anorexia is an isolating experience, perhaps even more so than for a female.

The chances of misdiagnosis are greater owing to the stereotype that it is a 'female thing' (see chapter 1) and if the diagnosis is made correctly the man still has to experience the stigma and consequent humiliation of being so conspicuous. Many treatment programmes are geared towards females only (in the groups that are taken etc) and although things can be adapted to treat men this can only add to the feeling of being alone with such a frightening condition.

Steve is still alone with his illness and finds it hard to even try professional treatment after all the wasted attempts before. He finds weekends the hardest and the anorexic behaviours are overwhelmingly powerful. Every time he hurts himself he is filled with regret *'I promise myself that I will never do this again, but of course I do'*, the illness is so strong that he is unable to help himself, and yet he does not feel that he can be helped by anyone else. Steve still has hope though and that fact alone is enough to mean that someday he will reach recovery.

'Please go away anorexia'.

Lucy ...

'Don't lose sight of the fact that the illness destroys lives.'

The early stages of being in recovery have proved to be a real roller coaster ride for Lucy, positive and full of hope one day then plunging back down low the next. Although the low days are difficult to cope with, she is determined to keep moving through, as she knows that it will be worth it.

Lucy is very intelligent, charming and extremely sensitive and caring, until early this year, however, she was very much in the grip of the illness that was destroying her and her life. She was in the middle of her degree when things became too serious and she had to leave to go into treatment, it is strange to say that it was the best decision she could have made.

Now, living in recovery she has decided not to return to finish her degree but instead has begun her nurses training, something she is incredibly passionate about. Not only did the treatment save her life but it gave her the opportunity to evaluate it and without the illness she was able to see what she really wanted to do and had the strength to go for it *'I am so, so happy and I really cannot wait – I have never been more sure about anything in my life'*.

Although treatment is a very intensive period of therapy and a massive learning process, it is merely the beginning of dealing with life in recovery, which must be worked at every day. On discharge from hospital it would be great if it could be believed that every patient was cured, without threat of relapse or any remnant of the illness. Unfortunately with eating disorders this is simply not possible (at least not with current treatment methods) and *'although hospital may not have been enough, it began to lay the foundations and you can lay more and build on them'*.

There is by no means a guarantee that on leaving hospital the patient will be able to go about their lives without any further problem, the illness is so complex and often of lengthy duration that treatment must be continued well after discharge.

This is something that Lucy has had to accept through her months of life in recovery as although she is extremely positive, there have been real struggles since reaching recovery and she knows how important it is to keep moving forward *'I had a 'blip' about a month prior to leaving hospital (during a long term treatment programme) during which everything felt like it was falling apart and spiralling out of control. I just wanted to rest from constantly fighting'*. On this, most recent occasion she was able to see what was happening and pull herself back before the illness really took hold again, the time before this she was not so strong however. *'I let go and gradually let the 'behaviours' creep back in and before I knew it I was bang in the middle of a full blown relapse and boy did I regret that'* to prevent relapse it is essential to remain aware of what is going on and to remember what has been achieved by coming so far.

The nature of the illness is such that if during recovery, the person becomes vulnerable a relapse can happen very, very quickly. Indeed returning to the illness can often seem very appealing, as bizarre as that may seem to the observer *'there will be times when I am confronted by my triggers, when I am tired and the strength to fight is waning, when I am feeling the pull back to part or all of the illness so strongly'.*

Remaining in recovery requires constant effort and sometimes it is so difficult, seems so impossible that it really can feel that it is *'far too much like hard work and not really worth it'.* Such thoughts are of course to be expected when things are tough, it is how those thoughts are handled that is the real test.

Lucy holds on to the belief that times when she feels that way may be a regular occurrence in the early stages of life in recovery *'they will be fewer in the future hopefully and I will not regret staying well'.* She knows that even though the pull of the illness is very strong at times *'without a doubt I would regret relapsing, however appealing it may seem at the time'.* The illness could only ever provide short-term release from the pain of dealing with situations, thoughts and feelings, and after a brief period Lucy knows that she would want *'to be normal again and by then it would be too late and I would have to go through the whole recovery process again'.*

Learning to live in recovery is unbelievably hard but sadly there are no short cuts and only time and determination will keep the person well, Lucy is adamant that it is possible and it is worth it.

'Hospital treatment was not the end, it was the beginning and it is up to me now to put that beginning to good use.'

Kate ...

'I hope that with help from others and the willpower from inside me I will eventually reach recovery and live the life I deserve'.

It is often believed by those suffering from an eating disorder, and sometimes those around them that there is no real threat of serious medical complication, at least not until the person is much older.

Kate is proof that such immortality is not granted to people with eating disorders any more than it is to anyone else. She is bright, caring and has a superb sense of humour which is just one of the personality traits that make her such excellent company. Kate has, however, suffered from anorexia for many years to such a severe extent that the physical consequences have been very serious – almost fatal.

Kate's first memories are of attending nursery school *'I remember feeling very anxious about it and I never really felt very eager to go in'* saying goodbye to her mum was a daily ordeal. After a while however, she was able to settle and when she moved up to the primary school she made some friendships that were to last throughout the years at primary school. Kate enjoyed primary school and worked hard, she was also well behaved and got on well with the teachers – in short, for the first few years there were no problems.

Things changed in the last years of primary school when Kate's mum felt that she lacked mathematical ability *'she got a home tutor to give me extra lessons after school once a week'*. Although this was done with the best of intentions, it was unfortunately one of the first things that made Kate really doubt herself *'this made me feel really bad about myself and I felt so much lower or lesser than my sister who is younger than me'*. Although sibling rivalry is a fairly normal occurrence in families, to Kate it was exceptionally hard to cope with *'I felt stupid and no good at anything I did or tried to do'*. To everyone else Kate needed a little extra help in one school subject, to her it meant that she was unable to achieve in anything.

She started secondary school successfully but not happily, although she made friends she did not really feel comfortable with them *'I didn't always feel like they all liked me very much because I wasn't like them'* despite not really having proof of this or really understanding the feeling *'for some reason I felt different and as if I didn't belong'*.

In 1993 Kate had what she describes as *'the best time of my life'*, performing in Joseph and the Amazing Technicolour Dreamcoat at the London Palladium as part of her school choir. The contract lasted 3 months and it was a marvellous experience for her *'that was the last time I was truly happy'*.

By 1994 Kate was becomingly increasingly aware of her weight and through her dance classes was constantly being reminded of her weight and shape compared to her peers *'my dancing partner was the ideal physique of a ballerina and was obviously better than me at dancing too'*. Kate's mum had taught her to dance from the age of 3 and this was something that added to the pressure she was increasingly feeling *'I couldn't help but feel as if I was never good enough for her'*.

Over the period of about 6 months Kate made *'a desperate attempt to lose enough weight to be just like her'*. To begin with the weight loss brought success and admiring comments, but Kate was unable to enjoy them as she had another issue to face, *'growing up'*. She was ill prepared for the changes to her body that were going on *'I was scared, confused and frightened. No one had explained to me what was going on inside my body or on the outside'*.

Lack of knowledge is always nerve wracking but when things are happening to a person's own body which they do not understand, it is very frightening. Kate's main concern was the onset of periods *'I didn't know what to do when I started them, who to ask for help'* she spent months in fear and anticipation as to when the dreaded moment would come. When it finally happened, she burst into tears out of sheer panic and blurted it out to her Mum, *'she gave me a cuddle and some sympathetic words of comfort which I much appreciated but I could have benefited from a proper explanation'.*

To experience such a major life event without understanding was very hard for Kate to deal with. During the following few months, her body shape changed and developed, it was hard to accept *'I hated myself and my sisters both picked on me about it they teased me about my new body shape, my new adolescent appearance'.* To them it was a joke, Kate felt even worse about herself and continued to lose weight, current thinking has suggested that if children did not know about the calorie content of foods there would be less incidence of eating disorders in young people, Kate had never even heard of a calorie! Gradually she lost more weight than she originally intended and people began to worry, she liked herself better *'my bloated stomach, my breasts, my new figure had disappeared, my periods stopped'* all the things that she perceived to be the cause of her feeling bad had been brought to an end and this provided a huge sense of relief.

By early 1995 Kate was looking extremely thin but nobody mentioned that she may be anorexic, she did not even see a doctor *'I suppose I felt great really, I was in control. In control of my body and what my body was living off'.* All the feelings of inadequacy she had felt through the previous years had vanished, masked by the immense strength of an illness that was, in fact, taking over her and her life. Kate did not see it that way; she believed that for the first time she had found something that was truly hers, over which no one had any influence.

'As soon as people tried to take it away from me I

became scared, angry and wanting to gain even more control' things escalated to a dangerous level and her parents recognised there was a problem. They went through all the usual procedures, Kate saw various doctors and was eventually diagnosed with anorexia. In June 1995, 3 days before her birthday, she was admitted to a treatment centre in Berkshire where she stayed for a year and a half. The treatment programme consisted of individual psychotherapy, family therapy and groups, unfortunately things did not progress *'I don't think that within myself that I was ready to leave my anorexia behind, I experienced no feelings of willpower or determination to get better at all'.*

When Kate was discharged in 1996 it was due to the fact that there had been no improvement in her condition and the centre felt that they could help her no further. After leaving, Kate went to live with her Grandparents for a while because living with her immediate family was not working. She thought that life, including her eating habits, would be a lot easier if they were apart. Whilst living with her Grandparents, between September 1996 and February 1997, Kate worked as an assistant at a local nursery mainly to keep herself occupied.

Unfortunately neither tactic really helped as the weight continued to fall off; in the February of 1997 she was admitted to what she describes as *'utter hell'*. This was a clinic in north London (quite a famous one in fact) where Kate was *'fed for 6 months and at the end of August when I was at a weight that was unbearable for me to cope with but was healthy, I was simply discharged back home'*. This was an extremely dangerous time as Kate was still very much in the grip of the illness and the main focuses - her self-hatred, her weight and shape, were more prominent than ever. *'I was deeply unhappy and ashamed of my appearance, slowly the weight fell off once more'* Kate made great efforts to take control of her life in a positive way, however, and managed to enrol on a college course to do a diploma in Nursery Nursing and she made new friends. In spite of this the weight continued to fall off and Kate became more and more unhappy.

There was little question that she needed very real help and in March of 1998 was once again admitted to the clinic in north London, this was still not the kind of help she needed. Just as with her previous admission she was fed up to an acceptable weight, additionally however on this occasion her periods returned. This immediately set her right back and discounted any slight progress she may have made. When she turned 18 she was entitled to discharge herself and this is exactly what she did. *'Although I left with the attitude of success and determination to maintain my weight, things went wrong and again the weight was lost'* Kate knew that she was simply unable to prevent the influence of the illness taking over, even if she was full of resolve to stay healthy.

After this unsuccessful treatment Kate had to wait a long time for any kind of help, during which her weight continued to fall and her health deteriorated. She was finally given a place at Atkinson Morley's Hospital in Wimbledon, south London but the day prior to admission Kate collapsed at home. She was taken to her local general hospital where she had to be resuscitated *'it was terrible'*. After only a day she was transferred to Atkinson Morley's, it was probably considered that she would be better off with specialist staff as soon as possible. However, on arrival Kate collapsed again and was taken straight to St. George's general hospital in Tooting, she spent the next three weeks on an NG tube (a tube passed down the nose directly into the stomach) and gained a few kilos before being moved back to Atkinson Morley's.

It would seem however that the professionals concerned were not recognising just how fragile Kate was, how dangerous her condition. After only two or three days she collapsed again and was once more taken back to St. Georges where this time she spent two and a half months and gained 9 kilos by NG feeding. *'It was physically and mentally torturing for me, I was desperate to eat instead but they wouldn't let me'* to be an anorexic on a general ward is a very isolating experience *'I was deeply unhappy and lonely all of this time'.*

After reaching a more medically safe weight Kate was allowed to return to Atkinson Morley's. This weight was still very low however so it was imperative that Kate completed a programme that aims to reach and maintain a safe weight, although not a normal, healthy weight. She managed to achieve this through individual keywork sessions alone, no therapy whatsoever – still she had no understanding of what was really going on and was discharged back to her own environment with the anorexic thoughts and feelings still in place.

At the time of writing, Kate was once again in hospital and is now at what she considers to be the most difficult stage of living with the illness *'I desperately want to live life without anorexia, yet it continues to control me in any way it can and continues to make me so unhappy'.* There is now no doubt in Kate's mind that she wants to be well and live a real life, *'I have not had much chance to experience life or gain much from life yet as I've spent so many years controlled by such a terrible, horrible illness'.* There should, from her having hope alone, also be no doubt in her mind that she will reach recovery. In the past she has not been ready to fight it and live her life free from it, now she knows that she wants to, that fact alone is more hope for her future than there has ever been before.

'I will eventually reach recovery, I just need to find the way to achieving it and the right place for me in which to achieve the life I deserve'.

Evelyn ...

'Keep trusting and believing, value yourself and fight for your happiness.'

There is often the view that when someone with an eating disorder is at a low weight it is then that they are most seriously ill, physically that may be the case but, once a normal weight is reached, mentally there are more serious problems than ever before. Evelyn has been through a very intensive treatment programme and has been in recovery for two years and has been at a normal weight for nearly three.

She is a truly wonderful person who has so many special gifts, one of which is the ability to be really honest – even when that honesty is hard to take. The recovery process is a long one and at times it appears as though things are not progressing at all, but it is incredibly important to *'trust the process'* and hold on to the belief that life in recovery is possible.

Having been ill for a long time Evelyn completed the recovery programme at Atkinson Morley's hospital in Wimbledon London, a treatment that she firmly believes saved her life. However, she has found the months since discharge the hardest of all *'the biggest gap in help for eating disorders is the absence of guidance, information and knowledge of everything that comes after the recovery of weight, normal eating and discharge from hospital'* although Evelyn received some follow up treatment it was only two, one hour sessions which is not enough.

'This is when the true recovery process begins, the hardest journey of all and the make or break time' no one ever mentioned just how much of a struggle it would be to stay well and become truly free from the confines of the illness. At this time when Evelyn was really struggling and felt most helpless she could not find anything to help *'all the books stopped just where I needed them to begin'*. She sees a certain irony in this however, when she was underweight and could not use or did not want the help *'they were throwing it at me left, right and centre and yet when I reached a healthy weight and felt like I was going to pieces mentally, I was begging for help and couldn't find anything'*.

Evelyn believes it is little wonder that the majority of people attempting to reach recovery from an eating disorder relapse, the situation feels so desperate and it is easy to despair *'I desperately wanted to recover and felt like I was doomed to relapse because I couldn't get the help I needed'*. It is important to recognise how incredibly strong the pull of the illness can be when the person is vulnerable *'without help at this point relapse is virtually guaranteed'*. This is a terrifying prospect, to go through the horror of the treatment programme and the pain of weight gain and therapy only to relapse due to lack of help after discharge was unbearable for Evelyn, and undoubtedly any one else in recovery. She was extremely lucky however as after months of begging her consultant she was finally referred to *'a brilliant therapist who saved my life and my sanity'*.

Evelyn is well aware that this does not happen for all people in recovery and she very nearly fell apart again in the time before the referral *'there is no point dumping the person right back where they left life and became ill, i.e. at a normal weight with all the feelings and mess they had escaped from'*. The person may be determined to stay well, as Evelyn was (is) but it is so hard to do in the cold reality of real life *'any person in recovery needs guidance and skills to cope this time in new, undamaging ways'* she knows for certain that if not, the majority will be unable to do anything other than cope in the only way they know how i.e. using food, self – harm and other self destructive behaviours. Evelyn believes that an essential fact that often goes unnoticed is that *'physically you are well but inside you are the most unwell you have ever been'*.

Through her own experience of different treatments Evelyn is well aware of what is needed to reach recovery, and those things are a far cry from treatment she received prior to Atkinson Morley's. Her admission to a general hospital where she was tube fed and given 4 meals a day was an experience she regards as *'one of the most damaging of my life'*. This was not due to the feeding, although that was very difficult and painful, but to the treatment of her by the nurses who were *'for the 4 months I was there, eternally cruel and hurtful'*. At a time when Evelyn desperately needed care and understanding she was met with hostility and ignorance.

'They destroyed my spirit and innocence and my trust in humans who I thought would care for me and help me get better' they humiliated her, shouted at her and made her cry so much she is unable to describe it. These people who are classed as being in a caring profession made Evelyn believe she was worthless, hateful and made her ashamed and even more despairing than she was anyway. *'They kept my phone calls from me and sent my friends away leaving me alone and feeling completely abandoned'* she was on a ward with three elderly ladies who slept most of the time and the only window faced a grey wall. She wasn't allowed out of bed at all and got shouted at if she even stuck a toe out, although she believes it was *'just as well that I couldn't go anywhere as I was suicidal for most of my time there, I used to plan how I could escape or get enough tablets'* it is little wonder that she felt this way when she was so ill to begin with and then was ignored and treated with disgust.

Although Evelyn was desperate for help, she was thought of as being the stereotype of an anorexic and was consequently accused of all sorts of behaviours and manipulations *'I tried so hard to be good and cheerful and kind but they had already judged me'*. She became afraid to even pull the bell cord for a commode because every time she asked for anything she got shouted at, *'I was treated like a naughty child who was taking up their time and bed space, no respect or kindness ever'*. The domestic staff and a few of the agency auxillaries treated her more decently; she feels that without them she could not have survived those months.

The experience was still giving her nightmares a year later and Evelyn still experiences feelings of panic and of being *'unsafe'* around nurses, *'I can never trust them, I feel paranoid and I am never relaxed when in hospitals'* this is a thoroughly understandable reaction to a group of people that so totally misrepresented their profession and as individuals were so cruel. *'It broke my heart and still does even now, to think of myself and how trusting and innocent I was when I went in'* understandably Evelyn was also angry and frustrated that they were allowed to treat her that way. Even now it still hurts and she still feels so very angry *'in all truth I don't think, even in the illness, I was as depressed and unhappy as I was in there, nor have I ever felt so alone'* and these feelings were caused in a hospital – the place where anyone should be sure of being cared for.

Evelyn was also admitted to psychiatric hospitals on three different occasions, two specifically for anorexia, the other for suicidal tendencies and self-harm which occurred when she was not using food so much to cope.   She does not see that this kind of 'treatment' is of any use at all, *'nurses didn't have time or training to help or understand, all the patients were mostly left to our own devices and there were no groups, therapy or anything, just ward round once a week'*. The only remote benefit she can identify is that it did provide some confinement and took off the pressures of the outside world, although the boredom of having nothing to do all day often intensified the depression. *'We were like cattle, always being herded somewhere – queuing up for tablets and food over which we had no say'* there was little consultation regarding treatment and Evelyn witnessed many disturbing incidents involving patients who *'have no voice and seemingly have no rights, who are treated like numbers not humans with intelligence and feelings. The treatment of patients in psychiatric medicine is often inhumane and cruel'*.

Outpatient treatment came next and this was not particularly helpful either, Evelyn saw SHOs on six monthly rotations *'I was just beginning to build up trust when they would leave and I had to start all over with a new one'*. To make this situation worse, they lacked training and understanding of eating disorders. Some of them only wanted to give drugs as they thought that *'the disorder was the problem not a symptom, i.e. weight and tablets would fix it'*, others appeared to not be interested in psychiatry at all and *'were only there because they had to be and were therefore unsympathetic'*. There was one therapist who was excellent and did really useful and helpful exercises on body image and work on Evelyn's family etc. The sessions with her really helped, but she left after six months leaving Evelyn even more frustrated, depressed and despairing.

It wasn't until she reached what she terms *'rock bottom'* nearly two years after her first GP referral that the Consultant suggested that Evelyn could consider a referral to St. Georges in London (of which the Atkinson Morley's Unit, mentioned previously, is a part). *'I was terrified but I was prepared to do whatever it took, I saw no other option'*, Evelyn accepted that the illness needed a strict programme if any treatment was to work *'I had to totally give up control of it, half-way methods hadn't worked'*.

At this time Evelyn was the worst she had ever been mentally and was rapidly deteriorating physically too, *'I had hit the point where it wasn't giving me anything anymore, it wasn't keeping me safe, it wasn't working'* in her opinion this is an important point that a sufferer has to hit before they can get better. *'I hadn't been able or ready to give it up before because I still needed it and it was still serving its purpose, I needed it to cope'* it must be hard for the outsider to comprehend that something so destructive could serve any purpose at all but for a time, often a long time, it does. Evelyn had reached the place where it didn't serve any purpose any more and all that was left was a terrifying illness that was destroying her *'I was desperate and I couldn't take the hell anymore'*. She believes she was *'so lucky'* to get a place on the programme and from the day of admission she has continued to feel extremely grateful.

Although Evelyn is able to acknowledge that she did the work, she knows that she could not have done it without the staff and the structure of the treatment, *'I remember crying and being so thankful over and over again for being there and for finally finding nurses and doctors who understood and knew what they were doing – at least most of the time!'*

Finally reaching life in recovery and surviving those 'treatments' that were potentially seriously damaging has given Evelyn great insight into what is really needed to reach recovery. In the first instance she believes that the person needs to get away, totally out of the role/environment/people where they became ill, or may be keeping them ill. It is essential that the person is totally focussed on themselves and are able to concentrate on their recovery without interference or duties or worrying about the feelings of others etc. *'I think that a period in hospital is pretty much essential to do this, you need to be contained and safe and not have the pressure of having to function in the outside world'.*

This state could be likened to going back to being a dependent baby, the person must give up total control of the illness to begin with *'as you grow you are given more control back – you give up control of feeding, protection etc'.* Evelyn believes that giving up the illness in the beginning is the easy part, although at the time that feels difficult enough – in actual fact it only gets harder as the process moves along. *'It is incredibly hard when you are supposedly 'recovered' i.e. been at a healthy weight for at least a year and you are getting your life back together'* there are so many demands in real life and the present as well as having to deal with the difficult thoughts, feelings and issues from the past that come with reaching recovery.

Evelyn considers the hardest work of all begins if the person takes the step of entering back into therapy at this point *'to really delve into your past issues and attempt to truly heal'.* The complicated process of making sense of issues that have been masked by an illness for so long can be extremely frightening and really tests the determination of the person to get well. *'Everyone can recover if they truly want it enough, but only you can do it – no one can make you better'* unfortunately reaching recovery from the depths of an eating disorder is not something that a person can lie back and have done to them *'you have to use every resource, use it anyway you can'*. It is not the case that the help offered/received will be perfect, it needs to be accepted and used to the best advantage it can *'if you wait around or reject anything you don't feel is perfect and just what you want –you'll be waiting forever'*.

Also it is necessary to ask who is it not perfect for? If the illness is trying to set some rules then it is already winning and the person does not stand a chance, in full recovery there can be no accommodation for the illness *'you cannot hang on to any of it or you will still be ruled by it'*. It is the difficult truth that *'a lot of the time it will feel as though you are going against everything your head is telling you, you have to do the complete opposite to what you want – or rather what your illness wants'* it is so hard but it is essential to trust and believe that the risk is worth it and it is the way to live in recovery.

'Trust the healing process' is a phrase Evelyn is constantly reaffirming to herself, in addition to this she finds it necessary and helpful to refer to a page she has written out entitled *'For the love of myself'*. She always keeps this near her and reads it whenever she feels that she is struggling, Evelyn believes that positive affirmations do work *'but they take rehearsal after rehearsal, even if you don't believe a word at first, you need to recondition your thinking and it will not happen overnight'*.

These affirmations will be different for each individual; amongst Evelyn's list are the following points; *'Be gentle with your pain, embrace it, it is a sign of healing.' 'The power is in the moment, not in the past or the future.' 'Open your heart and mind to the world and to love. You can't move forward, be who you want to be and thrive with pointless, negative thoughts of self-hatred. Don't' let them stop you from being all that you dream and long to be.'*

'Dare to be yourself and be real, no matter how frightening or threatening that may seem.'
'Don't fall into the comparison trap. Your needs, wants and feelings are as important as everyone else's.'
'If things are a problem to you, they are a problem – full stop. Don't minimise them.'

These maxims alone cannot heal but they can most certainly help give reassurance when things are particularly tough. Evelyn believes that in order to truly recover the person must take responsibility for their own recovery and healing, must do things to try and protect themselves from the triggers that can make the recovery process even harder. For example *'stop reading women's magazines, they only serve to make you feel uglier, fat inferior and inadequate – I hate them!!'* Although such magazines do not cause eating disorders (as has been claimed), to a person with feelings of low self-esteem and struggling with negative self-image they can intensify those feelings.

An important aspect of living in recovery is that it is a choice, *'I have to choose to be well every minute of every day'* there is no doubt that suffering from the illness is not a matter of choice but recovery requires such resolve to fight the illness that the person has to choose whether to keep fighting or give up. This is something that Evelyn believes everyone working for recovery needs to consider, *'never give up – just because you have a bad day or even a bad period it doesn't mean you have to relapse. You can always get back on track, take control again'*.

She readily admits that she never realised how difficult it would be to recover, when she was in the illness it felt unbearable but recovery has tested her inner strength more than she could have ever imagined. *'I had no idea that two years on I'd still be fighting so hard, nothing can prepare you for the reality of the recovery process'*.

Evelyn often struggles badly and it often feels so desperately complicated and confusing. *'I sometimes feel so distant from everyone else, like I'm on another planet completely. I often feel so raw, I want to cry my heart out but I can't'* there is still so much pain to go through even after hospital treatment *'I often think I can't go on feeling so low and hurting so much all the time'* but Evelyn's resolve to fight is still strong. She has somehow, through all the pain, found the inner strength to battle on and even when it gets extremely tough she holds on to the belief that she will stay in recovery. *'I have no choice but to keep going and battling. I have to keep on trusting because I can't go back and I can't stay where I am. I can only go forward'* she is without doubt that her life is destined for so much more than the illness.

The illness has taken a large portion of her life but she is determined not to let it take over forever, even though the recovery process is so hard she maintains the belief that *'however long it takes I will continue to 'trust the process', if something is this difficult it must be worth it'.*

In contributing to the book, it is by no means Evelyn's intention to discourage people from working towards recovery, as *'nothing takes away the past like the future'* and there is no joy to be found in a future that is dominated by such a horrendous, destructive illness.

Sufferers deserve to allow themselves the chance to live their lives free from the illness and free from whatever it is in the past and, or, the present that has given the illness its strength. However hard it may be, *'you will be okay, you will heal and you will be free'* keep fighting and believe and *'keep your heart open'.*

Evelyn is full of the type of resolve that will get her to the point where she is truly living in recovery but she is certain that this can be true of anyone with the illness. The hard work will be worth it and nothing can be worse than losing your life and your true self to the illness.

'I do believe that one day I will be completely free and well and that there is beauty within me'.

Chapter 4.   Witnessing the Suffering.

In addition to the horrendous, devastating effect the illness has on the person experiencing it; it also has a very similar effect on those close to the person. In some ways the fear, frustration, helplessness and guilt experienced by family and friends are just as painful as the feelings experienced by the individual.

Initially the illness gives the individual a sense of safety, a release from the things they simply cannot cope with, to those observing, the illness has no such saving grace. It is simply a bizarre, inexplicable thing, which is taking from them the person they love and consuming that person with hideous behaviours, thoughts and often grave physical consequences. There is no safety zone for those witnessing the destruction. There are few things more painful in life than having to watch someone you love hurting in a way that could ultimately kill them, eating disorders have the added factor that for a long time they go untreated/treatment is resisted.

A difficulty faced by those close to someone ill is the lack of information and support. Families are often left in a kind of limbo, not really understanding, not being able to help, feeling responsible and feeling very alone.

The feeling of isolation caused by their family member/friend suffering from an illness few people understand can be immense. There are family support networks for many other illnesses but eating disorders, it would seem, are simply not a priority. It is very difficult for families to face that not only are there complications in obtaining help for the individual but also they are not able to receive the help that they need.

The contributors to this chapter have done so in the hope that their own experience may help others in a similar position know that they are not alone and also to see that the hope of reaching life in recovery is not a false one. It is also hoped that the words of those who have been through it will give some help of not only how to help the person who is ill but also how to survive themselves.

Although the stories are all different, there are clear similarities, for example, the feelings experienced are very similar and the difficulty of enduring life with the illness is clear from all the contributors. The overall message is one of hope and although it may seem a long way off for many families, the truth is that reaching life in recovery is possible and the families do survive too.

First Shock, then Understanding...

'When I first found out, I felt very helpless'.

Bulimia is, in some ways, harder to identify than anorexia. For example, the person may maintain a relatively normal body weight and often they are able to give the appearance of eating normally. Over time, of course, there are physical symptoms that will become more obvious but by then the illness and associated behaviours could be firmly entrenched and this makes recovery even harder.

For Clare the revelation that her daughter was suffering from Bulimia came as a total shock, the fact that it had been going on for some time made the shock all the greater. Although it is the case that one of the facets of eating disorders is that they are kept as a carefully guarded secret, it is very hard for families to accept that they could have lived in the same house and not notice. Although Gemma, her daughter, was away at university at the time that she decided to tell her parents, she also told them that it had started well before she had left home. *'It was a complete surprise, we had absolutely no idea ... even when Gemma was at home we had no indication whatsoever'*, this is the first thing that Clare knows parents will have to deal with, accepting the fact that their child is ill – even though they did not see it.

Gemma was so secretive about the whole situation and this was very hard for Clare and her husband to deal with *'even after she had told us, she still kept a great deal from us'*. The fact that Gemma was able to tell her parents herself could have been seen as a very positive sign, i.e. at least she was acknowledging there was something wrong. However the shock, coupled with lack of knowledge about the illness made it very hard to feel anything but confused and, as with most parents, very worried. *'I felt very helpless knowing virtually nothing about the illness'* it is the case that the majority of people will only know the bare minimum about eating disorders unless they are faced with it as Clare was. *'I knew virtually nothing about the illness, I went to my own surgery but they knew little about the condition'* this response from the local GP surgery naturally caused Clare intensified feelings of helplessness.

It is often the case that local surgeries are unable to provide the much needed information, fortunately for Clare, the Sister there was able to give her the number of a society who provided her with some more information. This is something that Clare feels is very important, it is hard enough for a parent to accept that their child is ill without the added difficulty of not really knowing what is wrong or what they can do. As a parent it is the natural instinct to try and prevent their child experiencing any suffering, to find out that the child has been suffering without their knowing carries very difficult feelings for the parent. *'I still feel very upset that when she needed us most, we didn't even know'* there is something very discomforting for a parent to know of a situation where they are totally detached from what is happening to their child.

This was made even harder for Clare by the fact that it seemed Gemma *'also blamed us to some degree'* whether this blame was due to her parents not helping her or whether she felt they were contributors to the onset of her illness is not clear. Since she was away at university for a large portion of the time she was ill it would seem to many that it would be harsh for her to blame her parents for not knowing, however it is necessary to remember that the head of someone with an eating disorder does not always think rationally.

It is often the case that sufferers of eating disorders are actually crying out for help but just want someone else to notice rather than them having to say it out loud. If people don't notice, the sufferer can then feel very real resentment. For Gemma it may have been that something in her background with her parents/her position in the family was a trigger for her illness but without being able to explain this, her parents were left feeling guilty and responsible.

This was made even worse for Clare by the difficulty in finding any real help for Gemma, *'I found the lack of anyone who was able to really help her very frustrating'*. Gemma saw various professional people, most of who did not appear to be very helpful at all, in fact some were positively damaging. One counsellor in particular only seemed interested in *'how much she had been abused by us in her childhood'* this of course, made things even more difficult for Clare and her husband. They felt absolutely awful and even more responsible for Gemma's condition, even though they knew they had done nothing wrong. This situation was a dangerous waste of time and was a further cause of very negative feelings.

The provision of care/treatment specific to eating disorders seemed almost impossible to find, or at least gain access to, it seemed to Clare as though it was not really recognised as being a serious condition *'we have private health insurance but eating disorders are not covered'*, as time went on she became increasingly worried and she kept saying to her husband *'surely there must be someone who can do something'*.

Things finally came to a head when Gemma was admitted to hospital after an overdose; this was the turning point with regards to treatment. When she disclosed that she was suffering from bulimia she was referred to a psychologist, who specialised in treating the illness and she turned out to be *'wonderful, I feel we owe her a great deal'*. The block the illness was creating between Gemma and Clare was not eradicated immediately, *'despite my asking, it was a long time before Gemma would allow me to talk to her (the psychologist)'*. Clare believes that the therapist suggested that she came to see her too and Gemma, somewhat reluctantly, agreed. Thankfully this was absolutely the right thing to do, as it was *'a great help to both Gemma and myself'*. From this time things began to move forward for Gemma and Clare was given the hope that her daughter was really going to reach recovery.

After all the despair, the hopelessness and the worry there were finally signs of a real future, and indeed Gemma has gone a very long way towards really living in recovery. In August 1999 she married and in August 2000 she gave birth to her *'simply gorgeous'* baby boy, to have suffered with the horror of an eating disorder and then find real happiness is a wonderful thing.

For Clare it has brought massive relief *'obviously as a mum, I sincerely hope that Gemma never has to go through those years again'* it is a terrifying thought for a parent to consider that they may lose their child and having to watch that child suffer from a serious illness without anything being done to makes such a possibility even harder to bare.
'Fortunately she survived but things could easily have been very different'

Clare sees lack of understanding of the illness as being partly to blame for how long the illness can remain untreated *'I think that many people think the illness is a 'fad' of young girls, like being on a diet'*. This links to the belief that the illness is really only about weight and shape and that it is just part of teenage girls becoming more body conscious, if it were this simple, neither Gemma nor anyone else with the illness would suffer in secret or for so long.

Neither would anyone reach the point where they take an overdose.

Clare also believes there needs to be much more information and advice available for anyone who needs it, particularly for parents. She believes that the availability of this depends greatly on the area *'Cheltenham had very little to offer as I do not think doctors here have much awareness of the illness, in Cambridge (where Gemma was at university) it was easier'.* Clare also thinks that some information being provided in schools would be helpful and even simple things like all doctors' surgeries having available leaflets with advice and information could make all the difference to relatives/friends who want to help or at least to try and understand.

A further consideration is that, in Clare's view, there should be more clinics available for treatment of eating disorders, there seemed to be so few possibilities when Clare was trying to find help for Gemma. Through learning more about the illness, Clare is aware that there is the chance that one day Gemma may become ill again, *'I am not sure if one ever really recovers totally from this illness and I understand that given the wrong circumstances it can occur again'.* Whilst Clare and her husband will inevitably have this possibility at the back of their minds, Gemma has made such progress and has moved on to such a positive period of her life that the future certainly seems bright.

For Clare and the rest of the family, coming to terms with Gemma's illness has been very difficult and at times the feelings of helplessness and frustration were extremely hard to deal with. These are, of course, very natural feelings for the family of some one who is ill and the fact that Gemma kept it from them and then was reluctant to accept their involvement in her treatment made it even harder. Both Gemma and her family have come through it though and Clare believes that they all have the strength to continue to move forwards.

'I feel that she has gone a long way towards a real recovery and with the vital support of her family and friends, her good husband and simply gorgeous little boy, we have great hopes for her future'.

Allowing yourself to hurt too ...

'I'm angry that this wicked disease had to sink its claws into my sister'

Lily's older sister suffered from anorexia for over ten years, Lily who is four years younger, was not aware of what was going on for a long time but when she was it became one of the hardest things that she and her family had to cope with.

Being younger somehow made it harder for Lily as the norm is to look up to one's older siblings for guidance, advice etc but her sisters illness made her in need of Lily's help not the other way round. Her sister is now in recovery and things are looking much more positive but for a long time the pain was in some ways as great for Lily as it was for her sister.

To begin with there was not really anything that caused Lily concern, even though she began to notice things about her sister that were different. *'I can't remember the beginning but my first memory of her wasting figure was a silver necklace she wore for a while'* it is interesting that something that would seem insignificant to others has stayed fixed in Lily's memory for so long. *'The chain would never hang straight as chains did when my mum or other women wore them. Instead it lay in jagged curves over her prominent collarbone. The pendants sank into the well that had developed between the tendons at the base of the neck'* it was the smallest of signs for others to see and for a young girl it did not really mean anything *'at the time it was fascinating'*. Looking back on it, Lily cannot imagine how it did not worry her *'now the thought of it is terrifying'*.

It is only really with hindsight that Lily recognises just how ill her sister was becoming well before the 'official' diagnosis, *'now when I look back at photographs of when she was 15 or 16 it is obvious how fragile she became, I never saw that for myself at the time'*. It is hard for Lily to look at those photos now as the most noticeable thing about them *'was not her virtually skeletal appearance but her smile. It is only there in the curve of her lips, not in her eyes – they only look dark and lost'* it is possible to try and hide pain with a smile but if anyone looks into the eyes of someone who is suffering it is impossible to hide. What is even harder for Lily to deal with is the fact that she now knows that the dark, lost expression in the eyes *'showed only a small part of what she was feeling inside'*.

Whilst Lily is able to recognise that *'everyone hides his or her true feelings to some extent'* she firmly believes *'that everyone wears a mask to cover whatever it is we don't want the world to see'*. The art of concealment is one that seems to be an unavoidable part of being human, for Lily's sister it was more than just a part *'I just never knew that she must have worn her mask every day for so long'*.

It was only when people began to help her sister and she allowed herself to be helped *'that we saw the full horror of what lay behind that mask'*. Like most people, Lily has periods of feeling low and bad about herself, of feeling worthless and as though she can't get at grip on anything *'in recent months, these moments of panic and self doubt have been intensified with the knowledge or realisation that they could be something close to how someone I love so much must have felt constantly for so long'*. Making this connection may well be something that Lily would rather not have discovered, it is hard enough to imagine how another person is feeling when you know they are in pain, but when you are hurting in a way that must have been something close to that persons pain it makes it horribly real. This coupled with the wish that *'I would give anything to change that'* makes it difficult for Lily to come to terms with even though her sister is now in recovery.

The wish to change the past is one that many people have but Lily knows that her sisters past nearly meant she didn't have a future and so many of her destructive thoughts were fuelled by the illness, not by reality *'I want to take it all away so she never knew what it felt like to be disappointed in herself when no one else was'*.

Lily knows only too well how hard it is for families to bear the reality of just how serious the illness is, the desperate need to help when it seems impossible, the futile attempts to do something positive when it is rejected, the fading hope of recovery ever happening. Lily believes that all too often people ignore how much the illness hurts the family too, something that can make the horror even harder to deal with. She feels privileged that she did have someone in her life who reached out to her *'I remember the first time someone showed me that they knew I was hurting because she was'*, it was her first employer as a teenager who knew both Lily and her sister very well and for a long time was a very good friend to both of them. It is a funny thing that sometimes *'the people you least expect to, can make you think and feel the most'*, for so long Lily had thought only of her sister, what she could do for her and what she could make other people do for her and as she was leaving work, totally out of the blue, her employer said *'people don't realise how hard another persons pain is on those around them'*. Up until that point, Lily had been one of those people, she hadn't realised, hadn't allowed herself to express how much she was hurting, how hard to was to keep it together.

'To hear someone say it out loud with a smile that showed he really cared meant the world to me' this was from a person who only really knew the most basic facts. *'He had never seen her anguish at the dinner table, never heard our father shouting and slamming doors out of pure frustration because she couldn't eat or tell us why she was hurting'*. Nether the less, he was able to recognise Lily's pain and with those few words he let her know that she was not alone, *'that day he helped me cry so many tears that I didn't even*

realise I needed to release'.

Lily firmly believes that there needs to be more support for the families of those with the illness, obviously they need information and advice on what is going on and what to do but Lily highlights the need for more than that. Perhaps support networks with meetings etc (these are particularly lacking in rural areas), would mean that those having to cope with someone else's pain as well as their own would feel less isolated and would have an outlet for some part of the nightmare.

A further difficulty that Lily knows families have to bear is the need to find a reason when there is not an identifiable one *'I suppose it is human nature to want to place blame'.* From the moment that she knew her sister was ill and throughout her recovery, Lily has tried so hard to find the reason for her sister becoming ill but is now *'learning to accept that there is no one true reason for me to find, although logic tells me there must be for one person to suffer so much'.*

Lily shares the hope of all those involved with eating disorders that one day there will be an identifiable factor that explains why certain people suffer from this terrible illness. For the time being she is trying to accept that it, like any other illness, just happens. Lily feels much more than this confusion and frustration however, *'I still feel anger. I'm angry it took so long to bring my big sister back, I'm angry that she was denied so many of her precious years.'* Although others may see this as being misplaced, Lily feels anger at herself *'I'm angry that I was blindfolded by my own youth and ignorance and angry that I cannot turn the clock back and go to my sister every time she reached out and I didn't see'.* Perhaps more appropriately she is angry with others, those who she believes should have saved the pain earlier *'the medical profession had the age and knowledge that I lacked but didn't use it for so long'.*

The anger she feels is also on behalf of others *'I'm angry that this illness made my mother doubt the maternal gift her children know she has'* it is a desperately sad truth that the illness has such a profound affect on those around them as well as on the sufferer. Clearly this is a massive amount of anger for any one person to feel and yet Lily feels it just as intensely now as she did during the worst period.

However the feelings are not all negative, she also feels many positive things *'I am blessed, this illness did not take my sister away from me forever. We share the same blood and determination that says "no – you won't take me, you will not deny me the love I have been blessed with"'*. Her sister reaching recovery brought not only the obvious relief but also the reassurance that however powerful *'this purely evil illness'* may be, it has never won and in spite of how difficult the future might be, it never will.

Lily firmly believes that families of sufferers need to hang on to the truth about the person they love, no matter how ill they are the illness can only really take them away if those around them give up. Lily knows through her sisters experience that reaching recovery is possible if the sufferer is encouraged to believe in themselves and somehow find the strength to let others help them, and to help themselves. *'Despite the pain, suffering and torment this horror has caused it has never beaten any of us. Not while I can say how proud I am of my sister and how much I love her. Nothing can take that away although anorexia tried to for many years.'*

Lily also attributes this to the resolve of her sister, she was so ill for so long and never gave up, partly due to the love of her family. Anorexia is an illness with a great strength but it didn't take Lily's sister from her *'she wouldn't let it'*.

'I have never felt anger towards her, only towards the illness. I have never blamed her, only the illness.'

Such a Waste ...

'The real story is the loss of contribution of these people ...'

Through his life, and he is only 27, Ian has had the misfortune to know three victims of eating disorders, he does not mean misfortune in the sense of having known them but refers instead to *'the pain of seeing extraordinary people crippled by something beyond their control'*.

Indeed he feels honoured to have known all of them, a girlfriend, a friend and a sister. Each of these people had a period of their lives taken from them by the illness and Ian knows that he is not alone in the fact that it took time to realise the depth of the illness. He recognises that even if the behaviours begin consciously they very quickly seem to become involuntarily *'the challenge for anyone living with a sufferer is understanding that they cannot control their actions'*.

Ian knows that the natural reaction of trying to sit the person down and get them to eat a decent meal just will not work but he is quite ready to admit that he has had real trouble understanding the whole condition. *'For anyone as pragmatic as I am, the idea of self abuse is as difficult to relate to as someone from a foreign culture explaining an emotion I've never felt in a language I don't speak.'*

In a somewhat disturbing way he feels that the physical side of the illness can, in time, be adjusted to – even though it is not easy *'to know that a loved one spends their time on the edge of physical collapse'*. What is harder still is the fact that they actively exacerbate their predicament by causing themselves further harm, however, in spite of how hard it is *'confusion and disgust quickly turn to a need to help and support'*. The real difficulty comes with the realisation that one cannot help, frequently sufferers are secretive and dishonest about their condition *'often they are lying to themselves, let alone to you'*.

Also, as Ian has experienced, even if they will discuss it *'your logical, considered discourse and possibly their constructive replies, bare no relation to the problems they face or their future actions'*. Ian sees the impossibility of living with someone in the grip of an eating disorder is the growing certainty that no matter how *'worldly wise or in control of your own life you may be, you are almost useless to them'* having been close to three different individuals Ian perceives sufferers as being *'in an internal hell, totally beyond your reach'*. He is very ready to acknowledge that any distress suffered by him in witnessing the illness does not compare to the pain suffered by them, although he is very careful not to comment on this, as *'it is still impossible for me to completely understand'*.

In his opinion, the real tragedy of eating disorders is still grossly ignored, the media focus on the behaviours of individuals and their effects and the majority of people consider little more than this. Ian firmly believes that the loss of what these people could be, what they could give, if they were not/had not been ill. *'Each of the three I have known is attractive, intelligent and hugely talented. They should all have been confident young women with the world at their feet.'* He feels it is deeply wrong that they are denied all they should achieve through something beyond their control.

Ian is now able to believe that though one could argue that these illness begin as self inflicted, they do not proceed in this fashion *'these individuals are robbed of their lives while they suffer from these illnesses as unfairly as would an Olympic hopeful in a traffic accident or a great thinker suffering from dementia'*. Ian considers that if more people thought in this way then perhaps eating disorders would be seen in a more serious light, and sufferers would receive greater help and understanding a lot sooner. *'For this reason more than any other, eating disorders must be understood and treated as well as possible, as soon as possible'* it is true to say that the abilities and attributes of these special people should not be allowed to be lost.

Ian knows how hard eating disorders are to understand but he feels the sense of injustice most strongly and believes that is very important that others see it as such too.

'The current prevailing ignorance not only harms sufferers but makes victims of us all.'

The following two accounts are the thoughts and feelings of my parents, both perspectives are different but without a doubt the best way for me to show how an eating disorder affects others, is to present the views of the two people who were closest to me through mine.

Learning to Help ...

'Although I was not to know at the time, Anorexia had taken hold ...'

Richard is the father of three children, my brother, me and our younger sister. We are very similar looking *'tall and blond'* and each experienced the same childhood and upbringing. We were *'all born in the 1970's and enjoying what might be termed a happy childhood – room to play, toys, pets, holidays'*. Further to this we went on to similar achievements *'they learnt to play musical instruments, each enjoyed one sport or another and each had a successful education through to University'* but in spite of our many similarities we were also *'of such different character one might almost doubt the ancestors!'*

Above all, and possibly the hardest for a parent to take was that, apart from the normal childhood illnesses, all three of us had seemed totally healthy *'until almost a decade ago when my eldest daughter began to lose weight.'* Although there was no way of Dad knowing then, I was

135

already in the grip of anorexia *'and a happy, healthy young lady was gradually becoming more and more depressed'*.

At first Dad's reaction was typical to any parent, and that was to look for a cause, something to blame and there were several possible things that could be identified *'competition with siblings, the more introverted of the three, being unable to recognise her own successes and sinking deeper into depression, then the death of a much loved family pet to which she had been utterly devoted – almost to an obsessive level'*. It was almost too easy to apportion blame, to take the stiff upper lip English approach requiring someone to *'shake themselves out of it'* taking this approach prevented acknowledging that the problem could be serious and meant it could be almost dismissed.

Dad is now able to recognise that this approach was in fact contributing to the problem, a further contributor was the lack of understanding around my eating – as I was taking smaller and smaller portions, the *'insistence upon eating as if the selective refusal of food were merely awkwardness was, retrospectively, counterproductive'*. As the problem became more evident it became more obvious that help was needed, months of irregular visits to my G.P produced little more than treatment for depression, until it was *'appreciated that perhaps Anorexia was a more accurate diagnosis'*.

When I was then referred to the psychologists at the local general hospital, the realisation that I was really ill actually hit home *'as did the determination to ensure that treatment was relevant to the condition'*. It was very quickly realised by my Dad that real treatment by those who understood the condition was rare and certainly not present in our local health authority. *'It became obvious that Anorexia, as a condition, was a low priority within health care and that general practitioners, be they medical or psychological are ill equipped to deal with the matter'* as a parent he obviously found this rather hard to take.

For months depression remained the clinical diagnosis, appointments were few and far between and, quite contrary to what it was clear to see, it seemed to be considered that *'as long as the patient was alive, progress was being made'*. Dad began to feel that nothing would be done in time to help me and began to make efforts to secure proper treatment *'a furious exchange of letters took place, or rather one should say a furious stream of letters were sent – acknowledgements were few'*. He still finds it an extraordinary fact that *'requests for intervention from higher level and explanations of prognosis were met with a blank wall of silence'*, it appeared as though the health authority might only consider a referral to a specialist unit if *'life were threatened'*. My Dad understandably questions the decision that wasting away is not considered as life threatening! Furthermore he was also aware that my deepening depression was threatening my mental stability, although he had to acknowledge that it was only much later that he *'learned of the real thoughts of suicide my daughter entertained'*.

The nearest centre to where we lived specialising in treating the condition was *'a private establishment some 50 miles away'*; my sister found out about it through a magazine report and we visited under our own steam. It turned out to be a *'lovely establishment located in what had been a very large domestic house with extensive grounds'*. Although he knew that treatment would be long term, it helped that the environment would be as pleasant as possible and the treatment would be carried out by *'a very dedicated and sympathetic staff'*. An assessment was made and it was decided that I could be helped but the key ingredient in this was my own decision to fight the illness. I made this choice despite the fact that this would mean months away from home, family and more importantly, animals. *'This must have been an agonising decision for her to make as she was so home centred, but it was a real testament to her bravery, courage and determination to beat the devils in her head – as she termed it'* Dad knew that I wanted to recover and that was hope in itself, but I needed their help.

So at last there seemed to be hope, there was an agreement on treatment a place to go with people who cared and I was determined to succeed, things seemed to finally be moving in the right direction. Then disaster, again, the blank refusal of the health authority to fund the programme – no explanation other than the lack of priority. Yet again Dad was left with anger *'anger that health professionals, unable to provide the specialist care themselves should deny others from so doing'*. He also felt so angry that the official line was that the current treatment at the time was working, *'by this they meant that continued weight loss, increased depression and increasing fatigue leading to an inability to work'* was a show of progress!

More was clearly demanded, at this time Dad believed that the cause of the problem should take a back seat to the drive to ensure that proper decent treatment was to be found. Luckily at this time, my family became aware that the health service itself did have specialist care centres *'few and far between maybe, but they did exist'*. This at least gave further ammunition in demands for treatment, *'eventually there was a referral, an assessment and eventual placement in a unit, albeit some three hours travelling away'*. Dad firmly believes that it was ultimately only implied threats of legal action, citing a lack of professional care brought this about *'at no time did any 'generalists' admit that they did not have the specialist skills to assist'*.

What we experienced were professionals almost refusing to recognise what Dad later found out *'that anorexia is extraordinarily complicated'*. Dad is almost incredulous that *'at no time was there an appreciation that treatment needs to be centred upon inter-personal relationships, of building trust confidence and understanding'*. He also sees the so common practice of prescribing drug therapies as largely only a question of *'putting elastoplasts over the wound'*.

Dad firmly believes that any parent faced with this condition in their child, has to appreciate Anorexia does not have a high profile or priority within the general scheme of medical care *'specialist help is thin on the ground and has to be fought for'*. He knows through his own experience that, if nothing else, it demands many hours of letter writing, research, telephone calls and a determination to succeed *'even to the point of using the law/media if necessary'*. In Dad's experience, it seems that there is *'no right to treatment in its correct sense'* and yet another problem he sees is what could be called *'punishment by geography'* in that the more remote your location from centres of excellence *'the more you have to fight'*. It is rather disturbing to say that Dad sees this fight as not only being for a scarce resource but also with *'the wall of silence which surrounds health professionals when a perceived threat to competence or criticism of professional knowledge is made'*.

Dad finds it clearest to define my road to life in recovery as a series of battles which he personally, myself and the family together had to face. The first battle was to secure treatment, and the next (when this was achieved) was to work towards really understanding the nature of the illness and the part that parents could play in helping reach recovery. *'Thankfully real professional help was now at hand, along with considerable helpful literature'* Dad knew by this time that it was only by understanding that he would be in a position to help in a meaningful way. *'Support was key – but support which was positive'* and he needed to know how to provide this.

Although admission to a specialist treatment unit was exactly what I needed, he had little idea of how hard it would be for me in so many different ways. *'For my daughter, who was used to the outdoor life, the initial weeks of long bed rest, almost 'forced feeding' and the confines of an ageing hospital complete with seriously mentally ill patients must have been the stuff of nightmares'* and Dad was also aware that the distance from home added to the burden. It was essential to keep in regular contact *'by* telephone, letters, cards, messages on her pager – anything to break her monotony and to ensure that she knew there was care, support and encouragement', Dad also knew that visiting was important. Often he rearranged business schedules to ensure that at least an hour or two could be spent with me on a regular basis 'the roads and rail tracks to hospital became familiar routes'. Shops were scoured to provide activities, which would keep my mind active and yet focussed 'my lap top computer found itself on extended loan so that her passion for writing could continue'.

The third battle, essentially my own, slowly began to be won 'small stages but of huge significance'. In the long, incredibly hard struggle, finally positive changes were happening 'first, walks in the hospital grounds – a rock on the edge of a mundane field where we could sit and chat achieving huge prominence along with an illicit can of Diet Pepsi!'
As the treatment programme progressed, I was allowed out of the grounds and Dad accompanied me on short trips to the local town 'and then eventually the 'meal out' – never did a pizza achieve such high status.'

Gradually there was more and more independence and eventually I became a day patient, living in a hostel close to the hospital this gave me 'the reality of being normal – the ability to go shopping, to cook and eat her own food, to go out with friends, for meals and take expeditions to the "big city"'. Dad saw each of these small steps adding up to huge strides as my confidence returned and my self esteem rose as 'her appearance changed into once more that of a beautiful young lady'.

Much to my Dad's delight, my self-esteem took on a new aspect, 'she took it upon herself to ensure that others knew both of the condition and of the determination and bravery needed to beat it back'. My writing resulted in a national newspaper publishing a two-page feature about my life and treatment of the illness, and eventually culminated in a television appearance. This put me in touch with many others and added to the feeling of support I was offered, *'it also greatly enhanced her own view of herself and considerably highlighted the nature of the condition for a countrywide audience'*. Of course Dad realises that such avenues may not be open to all but he believes the story illustrates the importance of support and of encouraging sufferers of the condition to utilise their own personal strengths in a positive way. *'In my daughters case it was writing, but in the same hospital were young people with other talents – one a particularly skilled artist, and in many ways it was sad that they did not appear to have the encouragement to build on these in the same way'* even if they had the encouragement, the illness prevented them from following it.

The fourth battle was, however, for both parents. It was the battle to understand not only the condition itself, but also the part each may, unwittingly, have played in the onset and development of the condition. Dad sees Anorexia as a response, it is not something that is caught from others with it's origins in a bacteria or virus, *'it is a response to condition; it is the result of perception, real or imaginary, of factors affecting the sufferer and it is quite clear that these can often be deep seated'*.

My Dad knows that at first there is a tendency to believe that *'it is nothing to do with me'* and to seek to blame elsewhere *'school, perhaps bullying, friends who do not live up to expectations, animals who inconveniently do not live forever!'* What turned out to be equally important to the individual counselling I received, were the sessions of family therapy both with individual family members and the family group. Dad will now admit to a large degree of scepticism, but it soon became apparent to him that not only were these sessions a means to understand the problems of the illness *'but they were also essential in helping to establish at least part of the cause and to clarify matters which had been clearly causing considerable confusion in the minds of both my daughter and other family members'*. Dad recognises that it was through the family therapy that he began to appreciate that issues, which may be *'dismissed as almost everyday occurrences by some, had been interpreted in profoundly different ways by others'*. Such events had clearly added significantly to both the stress and ultimately depression experienced by me increasing the intensity of my illness. This realisation helped not only in offering the right support, but has also led to *'a fundamental reappraisal of thinking and actions'*.

In a career such as Dad's where others rely heavily on him to be *'right'* and to take decisions rapidly in a context where they might affect lives deeply, *'the lessons were hard to take on board.'* One of the most significant things that Dad recognises as a result of these sessions was that *'not only did we learn important things about each other but of much more value, about ourselves.'*

He firmly believes that Anorexia in all its forms has to be taken more seriously than it is at present, *'the symptoms are a sign, an explicit sign that somewhere relationships, perceptions and interpretations have reached a dangerous point and one where real physical harm could result'*. Dad now knows that the individual often suffers alone but the cause is rarely wholly within the individual *'learning this lesson by those "around the case" is as significant as the 'cure' for the patient'*.

He is also adamant that it is vital that parents and friends appreciate that there is probably no definitive cure, *'more accurately the patient remains in remission – hopefully for a lifetime but to do so will rely constantly on the positive support of those surrounding them'*. Dad feels strongly that *'to have almost lost a daughter and then to have a daughter regained is a precious thing'* naturally this is something he is anxious to protect and through the course of my treatment he is in a better position than ever before to help and understand.

'The determination is not only to safeguard and support her but also to ensure that my own actions never cause the

"trigger to be pulled" in the future'.

Surviving the Roller Coaster.

'Of course I apportion blame to myself, how can I not?'

Sue, my Mum, lived with me for all the years of my eating disorder (with the exception of weeks at college), some of the time with her knowledge, a long time without. She readily admits that contributing to this book was far from easy *'it is so difficult to attempt to recall my thoughts and feelings about my daughter and the anorexia we have all lived with for so long'*. Indeed she put off contributing for a long time as there is so much pain involved in the memories but also because she has the whole of our lives documented in diaries *'I must select "snapshots" in the first instance'*.

'You must not feel guilty' were words said to Mum by a doctor at a private clinic for the treatment of eating disorders, it was the *'answer to our prayers, the surroundings, the people and their attitude seemed to offer the last chance of recovery'*. Mum is unable to understand how she is not to feel guilty, as the mother of a daughter who suffered with an illness for over 10 years, which could be genetic and is most certainly triggered by life events she believes that she *'must be accountable'*.

In spite of the reassurances of professionals and myself, she has, like most parents found the bearing of guilt most difficult. *'As I was adopted, I have no knowledge of my own hereditary and fear what I may have given to my middle child – alone it seems she has inherited more from me than my two other children'*. My brother has discussed with my mum his difficulty in understanding why it is that I experienced the same up bringing and circumstance to him and Helen (younger sister) and I became ill and they were able to cope. This is something that torments my mum terribly, *'my own mental state is often in turmoil and I fear this is my own legacy passed on to her'* although there is no proven evidence that eating disorders are genetic, it is an understandable fear for a parent.

We were a family of five but Mum describes the years of my illness were like *'another had moved in, Anorexia takes on an identity almost and will not be dismissed or evicted without an intense struggle'*, having lived with me through my illness and since reaching recovery mum has also seen that even when recovery has been established, *'it appears to be lurking/hovering, just waiting for an opportunity to reassert its insidious presence'*. This provides a constant source of concern for Mum, as it would for any parent who has been made aware of the possibility of relapse.

In remembering past events, Mum is first able to recall how my eating habits slowly changed. At the age of 11 I became vegetarian and as time went on I became more strict about it as I learnt more (I am now stricter than ever but I firmly believe this is the real me – nothing to do with the anorexia). This was the first time when food really became of any obvious focus to me and caused stress within the family, i.e. one person out of 5 eating differently and I was supposed to try out vegetarian recipes, this didn't happen and often I would just eat the vegetables if the others were eating meat. Soon after this I announced to my mum that I wanted to reduce my tummy *'if only she had waited, this would not have been necessary as she shot up in height reaching 5'8'''*, of course she was not to know that my reasons for weight loss were far more deep rooted than I ever let her know then.

Family life around the same time was not easy; indeed this would be a gross understatement, as for many years *'the outward appearance belied what went on "behind net curtains"'*. Mum finds it difficult, if not impossible to identify any one aspect that caused the problems *'strong personalities, pressure of work, money, sensitivity, ambition, frustration, irritation, fear, lack of self esteem and confidence, lack of demonstrative affection'* all these things, in varying degrees, Mum believes contributed to what she describes as *'the melting pot of the household creating effects for each member'*. With hindsight and newly acquired knowledge it is now possible for her to see *'how the seeds were sown for Katharine's mindset to develop and for her illness to grow'*.

In May 1989 Mum received a telephone call which acted as a stark wake up call *'the Head of House from school had told me they were all very concerned about Katharine, he mentioned an incident then added "she looks so sad these days and is so thin"'*, she acknowledges that she really knew *'just had not faced it'*. I had long since passed the age of her seeing me in the bath, I had a large, baggy school jumper and *'successfully managed not to eat with the family very much saying, "I'll get something later"'*. As the three of us all had activities at different times and my dad worked late or had meetings *'gradually the family round the table occurred less regularly'*, when it did it was often a cause of conflict either in 'normal' exchanges between Mum and Dad, Nick and Dad and later and more frequently me and Dad over what I was or was not eating.

And so it had begun, my Mum was aware that something was very wrong and yet she had no idea of how to deal with it, after that first phone call with school she said to my Dad *'we need help, I cannot deal with this'*. Sadly she recalls my Dad's response was *'we don't know there is a problem'*, at this time she felt very much alone with a situation she did not understand.

Mum has looked back at length over my childhood and there are certain things she knows became of major importance to me, *'throughout her childhood Katharine tried to be the peacemaker, for example, she would always do household tasks to avoid conflict. Her father's sporadic, inexplicable anger would cause us all to try and divert potential triggers – without success'* now Mum is able to recognise that this failure was extremely damaging to me, *'the dysfunctional family (that she so-named) drove her to move to her own world of internal turmoil'*.

145

When we acquired our Pony, Peter-Pan, *'by accident rather than by design'* Mum recognised that he very quickly became the *'major comfort in Katharine's troubled life'*. Not only did he receive the essential care but *'he had her company for hours as she committed herself to a perfect field, grooming, water troughs etc'* I was becoming increasingly focussed on giving him the best possible life I could, but it was more than just that and Mum later recognised this. *'He was her confidante and solace when all around was falling apart, he went through G.C.S.E, A Levels and college'* I am well aware that my whole family found this difficult to understand and Mum will readily acknowledge this too *'it was not just anthropomorphism, she felt a bond which none of us could appreciate until his death precipitated the last physical bout of anorexia'*.

This third bout eventually resulted in admission to hospital, *'this was not easily achieved'*. The clinic mentioned previously had a place for me in July, all that was needed was NHS funding *'I was assured this was possible if the GP and Psychiatrist agreed to support an application to the Fund Manager'*. Naturally Mum thought this would be straight forward as my GP was supportive and she had received a verbal agreement from the psychiatrist. Things were certainly not straight forward *'Katharine's psychiatrist suddenly declined to put pen to paper, of course, the fund manager – despite our protestations- could go no further'*, both my parents wrote repeatedly to all possible channels but the response was that placement in a private clinic would only be funded if no NHS treatment was available. *'We emphasised the treatment she was having was insufficient – the occasional visit to the psychiatrist was of no lasting value and in fact, more debilitating'* Mum recognised, as I was painfully aware, that having someone telling me that I would get better and that I was 'almost beautiful' was not really helping me to get better, after all, she could tell me that herself.

Eventually, I was referred to Atkinson Morley's Hospital in Wimbledon, Mum believes this was due to the persistence of her and my dad and I have to agree with this. After my Dad's initial denial, as Mum saw it, she no longer had to deal with the situation on her own, *'thankfully during the time we were trying to get treatment and throughout Katharine's hospital programme both of us seem to have worked together to support her'*.

To everyone's advantage my parents developed into what Mum has described as *'a surprising, post-divorce co-existence'* as opposed to *'warring parents'*, which she had feared, may be the case.

Places at the hospital were in great demand and after my initial assessments my admission date was brought forward, *'the case worker recognised that urgent admission was required, Katharine has since told me she was close to suicide'*. Mum remembers the initial visit to AMH as *'very difficult'* and this was for many reasons not least because of the environment that the hospital provided *'the contrast to the clinic was immeasurable; glass partitions, small bed spaces in shared rooms, emaciated, sad occupants'*. Not only was the environment difficult to take but the treatment programme was to be so tough and prescriptively structured it was *'a horrific regime, my daughter who spent at least 5 hours a day outside in a field was to be confined, not just indoors but in a small room with not even bathroom visits, in bed, consuming huge amounts of food (3000 calories), under supervision and with limited access to the telephone'* in spite of this we agreed to the admission *'what else had we? We had to trust that it would work'*.

Again Mum felt dreadful and responsible *'her Dad chided me for my attitude but fortunately Katharine was not too daunted by the contrast and began treatment in January 1999, nearly 6 months after we first tried to secure her treatment'*. On the day Mum and Dad drove me to Wimbledon, Mum felt even more guilt than ever before, coupled with a feeling of failure *'it was so hard for me to leave her, I felt I should have been able to help her more than I had done'*. She was also forced to realise that there are some things which cannot be fixed easily *'I could not love her more, but that is not always enough'*.

The moment when she returned home was when it really hit her what was going on *'returning to my empty house it was like a bereavement'* as a parent of someone with an eating disorder, facing the illness in it's extreme form (i.e. a hospital admission) is incredibly hard. *'My emotions, as throughout the illness, were so mixed, anger with self, frustration, helplessness, self pity, love and compassion for the sufferer are all over whelming'* these are by no means the only feelings experienced, my Mum believes that what is *'paramount are the almost indescribable feelings of hatred for the illness itself. It intruded on my daughter's life, almost killed her and is relentless, it never completely goes away'*. Although leaving me at hospital was hard Mum knew that it was our only hope and is now able to see that *'Katharine has been given the tools and the strength to fight it, thanks to the special people in AMH'.*

My treatment was not quite to the regime originally described due to a shortage of individual rooms, my Mum has often wondered if we would have been better if my phone calls had been more restricted. *'Although it would have been hard for us to not to speak to each other, I felt that a respite would have helped us both, however, there was not a day when she did not speak to me so I felt I was with her and yet with no guidance on my responses'.*   For a while Mum was filled with terror as I spoke as though I would leave, in February when I was told that my psychological problems were so great I would need longer than the normal programme time, this was almost as hard for Mum to hear as it was for me *'this was so distressing for us, it is hard knowing you have problems but to hear it from a professional is something very different'.*

The whole of my time in hospital was very difficult for Mum to deal with *'I felt so helpless and yet constant support was necessary'* the rigid programme seemed unrelenting and was made even more arduous for Mum (and she knows that it was true for the rest of the family too) by my comments such as 'if I stay' and stories of the continuous trials of fellow sufferers *one leaving after 4 days, others having endured varied hospital treatments since aged 8. Anguished cries could be heard when visiting and over the telephone too from the tortured inmates'.

Mum recalls one day in particular as being her worst memory from those 9 months, it was a week before my first visit home (which was only one day, not even overnight) and Mum was concerned about my travelling alone after being in the hospital for so long. She had phoned during the week and suggested that, as she was visiting for a therapy session on Friday, I could travel home with her and return on the Saturday (my Dad was travelling up to London so I would have had company for both journeys) *to me this seemed a reasonable request and I was lead to believe that it may be possible'.*

However, after much deliberation, those in charge decided against it and chose to tell me just before Mum arrived *'she was distraught, already at heightened tension, of course I reacted to this and that exacerbated her mood resulting in a violent thump on the glass panel in the corridor – the noise brought all the duty staff out and one came to speak to us'.* Mum was uncharacteristically assertive and said *'do you realise just how close she is to giving up and how close I am to taking her home with me now'* the nurse attempted to placate us and the family therapist continued the task. Travelling home however *'the tears came remorselessly – how could I have taken my beloved daughter to such a place? How could I leave her in that awful place? What could I have done to prevent any of it? What could I do now?'* Once again there were the feelings of guilt and desperation *'living with Katharine has been described as a roller coaster ride and I have described myself as 'shredded' on more than one occasion'.* Yet again she was desperately trying to find the cause *'how much of the ride can be attributed to the illness and how much to her inherent being, not to mention the environmental turmoil inflicted on her?'*

For many years my Mum and I have had what she terms *'a symbiotic relationship, becoming even more so at times of stress/depression from either one of us'*. Mum is now aware that in spite of how close our relationship was through the years of my illness *'there is much she kept hidden from me and that hurts'*. Mum is able to acknowledge now, however, that *'it is not possible to protect a loved one from everything that may cause pain, and we must all deal with our own devils'* it has been hard for Mum to accept this, especially as it was only when I had an article published that she knew I had had three bouts of Anorexia *'she had suffered during her college years and none of us knew – even though she was home some weekends. As far as we knew she had conquered the earlier 'problem' and any worries were the usual college years ones'*.

Mum is aware that there was no way they could have known and yet she can't help but reflect on how things were, and how they could have been *'how many family confrontations were because of this we will never know – we (Mum and Dad) had our own problems but sadly no proper communication, compassion or understanding existed'*. It was only during the family therapy sessions that any constructive interaction occurred but it has to be said that, for the sake of recovery it is far better late than never. *'Somehow Katharine's determination to beat Anorexia won in the end and she completed the structured programme – despite illness and accident the survivor in her had triumphed'*.

With the relief of reaching recovery came the realisation that at last there were positives *'through her time in the confined space, she taught herself to type, had two articles published, appeared on GMTV and began to learn Spanish'*. Mum (along with the rest of my family) were able to see even more than the hospital staff, how much I was/am changing *'from near suicide she has emerged to live the life she wants. The year before treatment, in my Christmas letter, she asked me to write that she was 'between lives' without explanation. Now we can announce with joy that life two is well underway'.* Mum now has all the distress and pain between us *'buried in my mind'* and she is working hard to accept that *'it is not good to dwell on the past unless to learn from it – I have many snapshots and echoes, Katharine could come out with such a wide range of comments, for example – "They won't let this kill me will they?" and "I'm fine, there's nothing wrong with me" or "I like bones" or "How can I sort myself out until you have sorted yourself out?" and "I'm sorry for … I need help"'* although Mum tries to keep these thoughts in their proper place, there is doubt she will ever really forget them.

Moving on is paramount for both Mum and myself *'one of her first outings from Hospital (other than to home) she met her future husband and it is with delight that I recall the moment when she tried on THE wedding dress! Both her sister and I had a lump in our throats and tingling eyes.'* My wedding was an amazing day for so many reasons and Mum believes that *'there was hardly a dry eye when she walked down the aisle – certainly not from those of us who know how close to death she came, not from the wasting away but from Anorexia driven suicide to release herself and us'.*

Worry and guilt are natural elements of parenting but Anorexia *'moves goal posts'* although Mum is well aware that reaching recovery is possible she is anxious that others should realise that it *'requires endurance from everyone involved'.* I knew I needed help and Mum is obviously relieved that, in spite of the problems, I received thorough treatment *'Katharine has vowed not to have to return to any treatment centre, she had that chance and her will kept her going'* Mum always holds on to the belief that the same strength will see me through recovery. She also recognises how lucky I was to have encountered the wonderful therapists and nursing staff, Mum is very aware of how important this is to recovery, there needs to be treatment but it needs to be with specialist staff who are trained to work with eating disorders.

Mum knows that acquiring such treatment is often not easy but she is adamant that it is essential for parents to be persistent and not give up, either on securing the proper treatment or certainly not on their child.

'Katharine acknowledges one therapist in particular for saving her life, words can not express what I feel for that person.'

Chapter 5.   Working Towards Recovery.

The complexity and severity of the illness is such that those who work with individuals in treatment have an enormous challenge ahead of them.

Regularly patients are admitted to general hospital wards or general psychiatry (see chapter 6) where the aim is more to manage them and preserve some degree of physical health by re-feeding rather than working with the individual to reach recovery. On a general ward the experience for the nursing staff can be extremely difficult. Often people in the depths of an eating disorder are incredibly manipulative, uncooperative and almost impossible to reason with. They can be rude, abusive even, and trying to help them is unbelievably hard. To say that nurses and doctors need patience is rather an understatement; the job can be very stressful and often unrewarding.

Working in an actual recovery unit can be a rather different experience to this however as there is the knowledge that the work is for recovery. Of course it is still one of the toughest forms of medical/psychiatric work as the illness will fight against the efforts to reach life in recovery but the satisfaction in seeing someone get there must be immense.

To work in such an area requires a certain type of character, I regularly used to say to other patients 'how can they bear to work here, we are so awful'. Even people who desperately want to reach recovery will often be very difficult and always extremely emotional. I have always marvelled at the patience of staff; the first unit I attended for assessment was the first time I had met a nurse who understood eating disorders, I said to her 'I can be really horrid' she simply smiled and replied 'that's perfectly ok'. In those three words she gave me more hope than I'd ever dared before, and that is the sort of person needed to work with people with eating disorders.

Mr. Chris Prestwood is one such person. At the time of writing Chris was the Nursing Manager for the St. Georges Trust Eating Disorders Service. He has worked within the area of Eating Disorders for many years in both private healthcare and the N.H.S. His understanding and insight into the illness can only have been achieved through real dedication and genuine interest I believe. Chris is very much involved with all matters regarding the treatment of eating disorders.

Chris describes the provision for the treatment of eating disorders in this country as depending largely on where the person seeking treatment lives, he considers it to be *'excellent in some places i.e. London but not so good in most other areas'*. There are centres of excellence in some other places, for example Birmingham and Leicester, but there is very poor provision in most parts of the country. *'N.H.S funding is an issue, but it is one that is very complicated'* minority services are unfortunately always going to be at the back of the queue compared to (for example) *'if I were walking home from work and broke my leg, treatment for that is very good'*. It is the case that this (and most probably any other) government are always going to have *'acute emergencies as their main health service priority'*.

There is money available however it is more how it is used that needs careful consideration. The existence of a *'contract culture'*, which has been in place for over 5 years, means that even in London the treatment received depends very much in which local authority the person lives. This *'contract culture'* is the term given to the arrangement local health authorities have with a healthcare trust that provide an eating disorders treatment service. It regards how much money the health authority has to put towards the treatment of eating disorders, the hospital in return then guarantees to treat however many people from that area that the money will cover.

Unfortunately this arrangement has produced some *'ridiculous situations'*. For example, Chris would argue that the treatment service he works in is the best in the country and yet a person living in that area needing treatment at the moment would not be able to receive it as the contract between the healthcare trust and the health authority has already been fulfilled this year. This means that for the next six months patients from the local area are unlikely to receive treatment at Harewood house (where the unit is based), even if they live just down the road! This type of crazy situation can cause serious problems; one of the key things about eating disorders is that treatment is most likely to be successful if it is received as early as possible. The lack of funding for treatment in a specialist unit particularly if a patient is unfortunate enough to be ready for treatment in the latter end of the financial year, may lead to very grave complications.

As a measure to try and combat this problem, more and more areas are setting up their own treatment services and (whilst some may be very good) it is often the case that these consist of little more than a consultant psychiatrist, who is not necessarily a specialist and therefore not trained specifically in the treatment of eating disorders, and a community psychiatric nurse (C.P.N). An hourly outpatient session once a week (twice if very lucky) is extremely unlikely to lead to a patient's recovery. Such a brief session is simply unable to deal with the thoughts, feelings and environment that the sufferer has to return to, i.e. the circumstance and triggers that have fuelled the illness. In fact, weekly sessions with no further support (as is often the case) can actually cause an increase in the feelings and consequently intensify the illness. Often, by the time the patient is referred to the inpatient service the thought processes and behaviours are so entrenched that it makes it very difficult to treat them and consequently very difficult for the patient to reach recovery. Additionally, of course, these small services are using much needed funds.

It would be so much better if the money were put into providing more places in specialist centres than spending it setting up and running an inadequate local treatment service. If people were referred to specialist inpatient units in the first place without the wasted, often damaging, time spent in ill-equipped local services it would make much better sense in terms of finance and treatment.

The way in which the contracts are made can also become complicated, for example, if a health authority had a contract for £200,000 (which could equate to eight inpatient beds over the course of the year) this finance would be based on previous experience of how much that local authority had used that allocation. In itself this appears to be nonsense since eating disorders (as with any other illness) do not necessarily appear in the numbers, or at the times that have been planned! If the money is not in place for a person living in one authority but it is for a patient from another, then it is sad to say that *'the clinical importance becomes almost secondary to financial importance'*. This is unfortunately true of most specialist units in all areas of medical and psychiatric treatment, the situation is made so much worse, however, by the fact that there are so few good eating disorders units around – the demand for places is so much greater.

The provision for the treatment of eating disorders is such that if a person lives in a certain area or their health authority has a good contract then receiving treatment is very easy, a straight forward referral and assessment is very often all that is needed with perhaps only a short wait. A good example of this is that, at the moment the very best place for a sufferer to live, for quick easy access to treatment, is Northern Ireland (not that one can plan these things!). Northern Ireland does not have any treatment units, only a very small outpatient service. Although this hardly sounds like the best arrangement, it is the case that they have a contract with the trust operating Harewood

House and after assessment and the need for inpatient treatment has been agreed, patients are sent straight over. There is none of the aforementioned delay whilst attempts at treatment are made in ill-equipped local services and they are virtually guaranteed admission to, arguably, the best treatment unit in the country. Therefore the treatment service for patients in Northern Ireland is brilliant as there is an excellent contract in place.

There is the idea that the ideal situation for the treatment of eating disorders would be that each local area would have an excellent, specialist, treatment service. This is simply not going to happen however and it could be seen as not necessarily being an ideal at all. As mentioned previously, if there are many treatment services then there needs to be many specialist trained staff and the resources available to provide all the emotional, psychological and practical help that is necessary to reach recovery. *'Although eating disorders are common, they are never going to be common enough for such a situation to occur'*, a much more realistic ideal would be that local health authorities work together to provide excellent, well resourced services that would mean *'there were 20 or so excellent centres dotted around so that everyone would have an excellent service around 60 miles away'.*

Despite the fact that it may seem unsympathetic to expect people to have to travel some mileage to receive treatment it is unfortunately the way things are. The best that can be hoped for is that at some point in the future, centres are more evenly spread. There is no doubt that it is very hard to leave home, and often travel a long way to a treatment centre, especially for someone who is very ill. However, it is the case that when a patient has reached the point when they are really ready for treatment and are desperate for help, they will be prepared to travel. A distance from home is a small price to pay in comparison to not receiving the best treatment available.

There is the other side to the coin however and that is treatment within the private sector. Interestingly, the reason why the private sector has reasonably good provision for the treatment of eating disorders is because *'they recognised, to put it bluntly, a gap in the market'*. Chris worked in the private sector because he felt that they would be able to set up a better treatment service there than in the N.H.S. at the time that proved to be right. Around that period there were so many areas trying to set up their own treatment services that trying to set up the contracts with the larger treatment services, as mentioned above, was very problematic. The result was that, rather than spend time in their local authority service, people were opting for private treatment.

A complication in how the private sector works, however, is that private treatment services are only set up where there is a big market for them. In London, for example, there may be a dozen private hospitals that do *'a reasonably good job of treating eating disorders'* and there are a couple in Birmingham and Manchester etc, but, if a person happened to have an eating disorder in Cornwall (for example) it is extremely unlikely that there would be any private treatment provision. A person could therefore be reliant on treatment services that are often inadequate.

Further to the size/specialist nature of treatment services, is it important to consider other factors that make up what is likely to be a successful treatment service. Chris is highly complimentary of a document published by the Eating Disorders Association that details with great specification the provision needed for a successful treatment service (see chapter 6). There are certain factors that are essential, Chris believes, in a service that is capable of helping patients reach recovery. The key issue is having a *'good eclectic approach'*, the illness is so complex that there are many areas that need to be considered when attempting to treat it. For example, ease of access to the service is vital, there is absolutely no point in having an excellent service if people are not aware it exists or simply cannot get into it – establishment of good contracts with local health authorities is essential. Owing to the contract culture (mentioned previously) it is extremely difficult to get really good treatment without a sound arrangement of this type.

Furthermore it is vital that focus is given to the emotional, psychological aspects as well as the practical re-feeding and giving up of behaviours.

There is a great need for psychotherapists who are specialists in eating disorders not just individual therapy. Although an individual therapist will be very good at getting people to talk and will no doubt be experienced at dealing with certain problems, the psychology of a person with an eating disorder is such that even the most experienced therapist needs to have had specialist training if they are to be able to help the person effectively.

It is important that the resources are available for occupational therapy, this type of therapy focuses on every day activities from work to establishing an ordinary daily routine. Occupational therapy can also involve activities such as meal cookery sessions as this is something that many sufferers may never have done for themselves. This type of practical help is vital if the patient is going to be able to enter into a normal life after treatment and can also help to prevent the likelihood of relapse. There really is *no point in having a brilliant treatment centre if patients are then sent out unable to deal with every day life … they will simply end up back in their illness'.*

Additionally the provision of family therapy with a good family therapist is very important, if not vital, to the patient's long-term recovery. Access to psychology and a variety of groups, such as psychodrama and art therapy, is also extremely beneficial to many patients. Provision should be made for a range of groups as some may help a number of patients and other groups will help others. If you were to ask a number of patients what was most helpful through treatment some may put psychodrama, for example, at the top whilst others would put it at the bottom. One could look at research into the usefulness of C.B.T (Cognitive Behavioural Therapy), which may state that it helped 60% of patients but that means that for the other 40% it was less helpful. Those 40 % would have found something else more beneficial to their treatment.

To make the assumption that treatment is as simple as one aspect is very misleading, if any patient was asked what was the most worthwhile part of their treatment they would obviously be able to say one thing but on closer consideration they would doubtless list any number of aspects of the treatment that contributed to their recovery. For some people, art therapy may be the aspect that helped most but for others it may be the thing that contributed least – the point of having a treatment programme that has a lot of aspects to it is that all the parts together will hopefully lead to the patient reaching recovery.

Taking this into account it is necessary to aim for a degree of flexibility in the service provision, the ideal scenario should be that service provider is able to *'gear the service around that patient not gear the patient around the treatment service that you're offering'*. That is to say that when a patient is referred they are treated as a true individual. This is very important in the treatment of eating disorders as every sufferer has a different experience with the illness and comes from a different background and circumstance. Different approaches help different people and a good treatment service must take this into account. If a treatment programme is too prescriptive, as many are, it is in danger of treating the person as their diagnosis, not as an individual.

Although the service Chris works for has a detailed treatment programme planned, changes are being made to increase flexibility and the programme is used as a structure to work from but there will (and, indeed, should) always be exceptions to this. For example, *'if there is a patient who has a young child and wants to eat with her child, what I don't want to hear nurses say is "you can't do that, it's only week 5, you can't do that till week 6"'.*

What is important for staff to bear in mind is that the illness is very manipulative and devious and therefore the staff need to be skilled to explore the situation with the patient in order to ensure that the request is not some form of avoidance but is for genuine, good reasons. Very prescriptive programmes are often relied upon by services operated by inexperienced staff; it is much easier from a nursing point of view to be able to say 'no, you can't do that this week, you can do it next week'. It removes the pressure of making decisions and is reassurance that they are doing what is believed to be the right thing. It takes skilled staff to really explore issues with a patient and it is possible that there can exist *'an incredibly well resourced eating disorders service with a team of inexperienced staff that doesn't help anyone with eating disorders'*.

Eating disorders are without doubt a specialist area and it is not possible to *'just set up a service and expect people to train on the job'*. There needs to be the resources for a good experienced nursing team, although there are many nurses who are very caring and try very hard to say and do the right things, it is just not possible to do if that nurse does not have true understanding of the illness, nor the knowledge of how to treat eating disorders.

If a service has a group of experienced staff in all areas then there should be a very good, effective, treatment service. This is the ideal however, as at the moment there are simply not enough specialist trained staff around – in fact there is *'not an eating disorders unit in the country that is fully staffed'*. The greatest shortage (as in all areas of the N.H.S) is of nurses, indeed it is the case that any nurses who are trained for working with eating disorders can literally choose where they want to work. A major problem with units finding staff is the distinct lack of training for working with eating disorders, this is of course true of any specialist area in the N.H.S.

A further problem is that the increase in local eating disorders services, as mentioned previously, has meant that there are many small services, which are rather appealing for nurses. Whilst anyone involved with treating eating disorders would *'welcome growth of services'*, this unfortunately has the effect of causing staff shortages, as there are simply not enough staff to go around.

This was not always the case, not too long ago if trained nurses got a position in a specialist unit they wanted to stay there and so there could develop a service run by trained, skilled and experienced staff. This of course also brought the benefits of a group of people who had worked together for some time and so knew how each other worked and whose skills would compliment each other. The result was very positive for both staff and patients.

The acquisition of knowledge is vital to the success of any specialist service, and yet it is hard to come by. For this reason, Chris is involved in setting up an M.S.C course so that anyone in the medical profession can have access to the training that they want and indeed is greatly needed. Another problem to contend with in effectively staffing units is the fact that, if asked which patients they most like to work with and put them in order of preference down to the one they like least – eating disorders patients are invariably at the bottom.

There is little reason to question why, to say the least, working with eating disorders patients is *'a very demanding job for a nurse'*, the nature of the illness and the behaviours it induces are so complex that the sufferers become very difficult characters often begging for help then immediately trying to reject it. It is a wonder that any nurse would want to specialise in eating disorders until one looks at the other side of the coin, whilst it is certainly a challenge, to help a patient reach recovery from such a destructive illness can produce very positive emotions.

It is true to say that working with eating disorders *'can be so rewarding when you do help people and you do see them get better ... remembering the patient they were '*, the change in a person who has been in the depths of the illness (often for many years) and works through to be in recovery is extraordinary. To be an integral part of that is something very special indeed, in spite of the unpleasantness and difficulties along the way, the reward and sense of satisfaction is enormous.

A further area which Chris sees as vital for treatment services to recognise, and act on, is the *'woefully inaccurate'* idea that *'when a patient reaches a reasonable weight, that's it'*. It is actually the case that *'reaching target weight is where a patient is at their worst as they've given up what has allowed them to cope for (often) many years'* it is at this point that the real work towards recovery can start. *'Only when someone has completely given up all their behaviours can they really start focussing on, not necessarily what caused their eating disorder, but what it is in their life that they are not so comfortable with'* this could be any number of different things or one major aspect of their life, for example *'something about themselves, their self esteem/self confidence or their situation in life or their position in the family etc'*. As one of the primary facets of an eating disorder is that it enables the person to block thoughts and feelings that are too difficult to deal with, for a service to simply re-feed the patient to a normal/safe weight and then consider them better is actually putting them in a far more vulnerable and potentially dangerous position than they were before.

As a consequence of this fact it is essential that the service provide good follow up treatment, *'for at least a year, ideally two'*. There cannot be much worth in a course of treatment which discharges a patient without the offer of support that could help them adjust to real life and could, in fact, prevent a relapse. It must not be assumed that acceptable body weight means the patient is better, *'if treating Anorexia is like reading a big book, then target weight is just the introduction'.* Any treatment service needs to provide a programme where there is a *'bonding together of the psychological, physical and practical aspects of the person and their life, which uses the skills of a team of staff'.*

Whilst self-help groups can be very useful and will help certain people, it is vital to recognise that (to coin a phrase from the treatment of drug and alcohol abuse) 'Anorexia is stronger than any one person', people with deeply set negative thoughts and feelings cannot beat it alone. This of course is true of so many things in life; alone some things are impossible, with help there is hope.

There are, of course, also complications that could hinder the effectiveness of a treatment service. For example, bad access to gaining treatment from the service can waste valuable time and could even exacerbate certain symptoms/behaviours – this means that the referral service needs to be swift and clear. As with any N.H.S service there can often be a lengthy assessment process followed by the inevitable waiting lists. It is therefore important that patients are properly assessed and diagnosed as early as possible. The diagnosis is often difficult as the illness causes sufferers to be very devious and manipulative; indeed it is often the case that people only see a doctor when dragged there by someone else. Although it should be great that they are seeing someone, if they have not gone willingly then they will not be forthcoming and may do all in their power to hide their secret. It is also all too easy for G.Ps' to dismiss the situation as 'rather paranoid, hysterical mothers' as they can't see a great deal wrong with the patient.

This often is due to the fact that G.Ps do not have the knowledge to know what to look for or the right questions to ask, often pure ignorance regarding the nature of the illness leads them to go on body weight alone, unaware of the fact that a sufferer can often be more unwell at a normal weight than those who are at a very low weight. Even using this criterion, if a person is wearing baggy clothes it is often difficult to tell what the body underneath is like and if that person is saying they are fine then the Doctor may not even weigh them.

Even if they do recognise that there is a problem many G.Ps simply do not know what to do, the average G.P *'has very little understanding of what eating disorders are about'*. Indeed this is true of a great number of the medical profession, even those in other areas of psychiatry, not just G.Ps. This is not necessarily their fault, and indeed it could be argued that *'we expect too much of our G.Ps'*.

Unfortunately, however, it is the case that *'the attitude of a lot of G.Ps needs to change to a certain extent'*, as (although this is not proven) it would seem to be the case that a large number of them, as with so many in the profession, dislike working with eating disorders patients. Indeed, as mentioned previously with regards to nursing staff, if asked their preference of illnesses to work with, it is most likely that eating disorders would be at the bottom along with drugs and alcohol abusers. This is due not least to the fact that people with eating disorders are inconsistent in their behaviour; asking for help and then rejecting or avoiding any help offered. For G.Ps who are always pushed for time and often for resources there must be a degree of frustration and irritation in a difficult patient with an illness they do not/cannot understand.

It is certainly not to be expected that every G.P is an expert on eating disorders, but to expect a situation where they have (and can provide) easy access to good information and advice is feasible. It is therefore essential for them to know what service provision is available and where they should be referring patients. Although it may be thought of as a good thing if all G.Ps were trained in treating eating disorders, it is actually far more realistic (and perhaps, more useful in the long term) that *'G.Ps be trained in having good, easy access to good information'*.

It is far better for G.Ps to refer patients on for specialist assessment immediately, before valuable time is wasted. Once a person has been referred they are more likely to receive an accurate diagnosis and the treatment they need. *'Communication, information and easy access'* are the key issues that G.Ps' should try to implement when considering their treatment of people with eating disorders.

It would appear, however, that the situation is gradually improving with G.Ps becoming more aware of the nature of the illness and being a lot more accepting of the need to make the necessary referral. It is essential that it continues to improve, however, not only due to the fact that G.Ps are always the first place any sufferer or anyone connected to them would go but also because they are the 'port of entry' to further treatment, there always has to be a G.P referral.

It is interesting, particularly for those working within eating disorders, to consider what the future may hold for research into and treatment of the illness. Chris believes it could be seen as a very positive move if the name of the illness were changed to *'illnesses of self-esteem'* as this may help to dispel the thinking that believes the illness is just about food, weight and shape. Indeed, it can be said that *'self-esteem and self-confidence are what eating disorders are all about'* although it is the case that every human being has *'issues regarding self-esteem and self-confidence, it's how we project those issues that is often the problem'*. It may seem that simply changing the name would have little effect on what people think, but it would perhaps be a move in the right direction.

With regards to research it is the case that *'there is an absolute plethora of research into eating disorders because, although (and as a clinician, this is rather annoying) clinicians dislike working with eating disorders, researchers love working with them!'* This is probably due to the fact that eating disorders *'seem to be something that everyone has a little bit of interest in'*, mainly because there is no definitive way of explaining or treating them.

There are a large number of researchers that look into various aspects of the illness, and end up appearing to be very learned and their findings are published in medical journals etc. Unfortunately if many of them were asked what eating disorders are actually all about, *'they wouldn't have a clue'*, however they are very good at research and they know the right way to conduct research. They will *'talk to clinicians to find out the right questions to ask and will go off and prove that psychodrama (for example) works well in inpatient units for 70% of patients'*. People will then read it and think it interesting when in actual fact, most of it is *'absolutely meaningless'*.

Regarding the future of research into the cause of eating disorders Chris considers that there will always be what could be termed as *'fashionable research'*, at the moment it is research into genetics. A number of researchers are keen to prove that eating disorders are caused by a person's genetic make-up although there is nothing conclusive as yet.

It may be the case that there will never be dramatic breakthrough in eating disorders research that provides a definitive cause or a great change in treatment. It is far more likely that *'we will generally pick up more and more information and gain more understanding'* and it could therefore be argued that other focuses for research may be far more useful.

With regards to treatment it would perhaps be far more beneficial to focus on qualitative research as opposed to the quantitative research that is so often favoured. For example, rather than investigating whether or not C.B.T was helpful, it would be far more productive to ask what aspects of C.B.T were helpful. To really gain useful insights through research it would be most productive to sit down with a patient and have an in-depth discussion about what was useful within any given part of their treatment. *' Sitting down with ten patients and asking them questions in detail would give more answers to questions regarding what is really needed in a good treatment centre than sending out hundreds of questionnaires asking 'what helped you the most? Psychotherapy, Psychodrama or Nursing (for example)'*, acquiring information from patients that is of practical use is, arguably, the best way of improving understanding of and provision for eating disorders.

At the moment there is rather a lot of research into what may cause eating disorders and very little into what really helps people reach recovery, for the benefit of those with the illness this is perhaps the wrong way round.

A factor that could be argued as being vital to the success of a treatment is something that is *'really immeasurable'* and therefore not looked at through research and that is when you have a situation where there are a group of staff working together very well and communicating very well. *'Having worked on a unit where this has been the case, I know that the treatment success rate is very good'*, when the opposite situation is true, however, where a couple of long term staff have left or there are some personal disagreements, the unit will not run anywhere near as effectively. This is a vitally important area that is simply ignored by researchers, as it is not neatly quantifiable as others aspects of treatment may be.

Chris also considers that it is interesting to consider the concept of eating disorders in men, something of which people are often unaware. Very often many men who would *'not be deemed as having problems, in fact have very serious issues with self esteem and are not comfortable with the person that they are'* in an effort to deal with this they often use avoidance methods such as binge drinking every weekend, for example. Women who eat and vomit are described as having an eating disorder; men who drink and vomit are termed as being a lad. There really is no difference; binge drinking can be a method of avoiding dealing with more complex issues just as is binge eating. This, of course, does not mean that all men who go out drinking have problems but it is an interesting fact that many do. Similar to this, many individuals with an eating disorder often have a father who has a drinking problem, i.e. can't get through the day without a drink and yet they cannot understand why their daughter won't eat, again it is really exactly the same problem.

Chris believes eating disorders should not be seen as *'something out there on their own but as something we can all relate to'*. It is true that if one talks to anyone at length about eating disorders and what they are all about, it is invariably not long before they will be finding aspects to which they can relate. *'The world is not made up of people who are ill and people who are well'* many people are actually on the very edge of an illness by the way they conduct themselves and how they live their life, it could be argued that everyone has unresolved issues and cope with them in various ways – not always healthy or productive. Interestingly, it is the case that people who go through an eating disorder (or other similar illness) are actually in a very privileged position in that they truly know themselves, not many people ever have the opportunity to take the time to analyse their own thoughts, feelings and actions.

After such an extreme experience it is also the case that people in recovery are able to see more about other people. Although they cannot always understand the behaviour of others, anymore than anyone else can, they are more likely than many to see the reasons behind it. As clichéd as it may sound, coming through such an all consuming, serious illness does indeed make a person stronger and far more aware of human nature in general, *'it is rather a provocative statement but perhaps everyone would be better off if they went through something like that'*.

Maybe if this were the case people would be far more aware of, and comfortable with, themselves and others with whom they come into contact. It may seem an extreme solution to the problems society experiences but there can be little question that in today's hectic society people in general do not feel able to take the time to deal with aspects of their life/themselves that are difficult, perhaps if people did this more there would be fewer people developing full blown emotional, psychological disorders. Of course this is not to say that the behaviour of others or self directly cause such disorders but there are always triggers that exacerbate the symptoms and the denial of difficult issues is certainly one such trigger.

Whilst eating disorders are very complex and often misunderstood, there are treatment services that are successfully treating them and general understanding (or at least limited knowledge) is slowly moving in the right direction. The hope is that gradually, all treatment services will work to develop the sort of service that is positive and helpful in all areas of the person's recovery and there will be an end to the sort of treatments that are actually detrimental.

The nature of the illness is such that the people that work with eating disorders patients need to be remarkably patient and calm, understanding yet firm. They are invariably this way and if properly trained, as Chris Prestwood strongly advocates, they are arguably among the most remarkable of all staff in any treatment area. To accept the difficulty of the challenge and face the pain and conflict every day is a job not to be envied, but anyone who has been cared for and helped by them are overwhelmingly grateful that they do it.

Chapter 6. The Right Treatment

Achieving the right treatment for eating disorders is by no means as straightforward as it is for many other illnesses, and certainly not as easy as it needs to be.

It cannot be emphasised enough that a delay in receiving treatment can be extremely damaging to the individual as it can result in a deepening of the condition – both in physical and psychological terms, which will make eventual treatment much more difficult. Not receiving treatment at all can prove catastrophic.

As mentioned previously, people with eating disorders are often given or referred for treatment, which is not at all helpful indeed often it can be most counterproductive. Eating disorders are so complex and serious that specialist treatment is essential if sufferers are to be helped towards recovery. All too often individuals are 'treated' by general practitioners/consultant psychiatrists (for example) who, whilst undoubtedly are very proficient in other areas, do not have the training, knowledge or skills to effectively treat the illness. It is vital that specialist treatment also involves specialist staff.

A major problem involving the provision of a successful treatment service is in distinguishing exactly what that service needs to be, what works for one person will not necessarily work for another. Although people with eating disorders can be diagnosed as either having Anorexia or Bulimia, the individual thoughts, feelings and behaviours vary enormously as does the experience of living through it.

As it may seem impossible to provide for all the varied needs of patients, it is important that there are certain aspects of any treatment service that are the same, but are adaptable to the needs of the individual (see also chapter 5). There has been much debate regarding the best ways of treating anorexia and bulimia and although there are still great discrepancies amongst treatment provision, steps are being made to improve the situation and develop some agreed method of care.

The Eating Disorders Association (EDA) is a charity set up to help people with anorexia or bulimia nervosa and offer support and information for their families and friends. Whilst providing support directly for those who need it, they are also involved in all areas relating to eating disorders – from increasing general understanding to working to improve the service provision.

As a result of the increased awareness of eating disorders, the EDA has heard from more and more people who are not satisfied with the treatment they have received. Also 'the need people have for information about eating disorders is demonstrated by the demand to the telephone help line run by the EDA. In 1994 EDA answered over 250 calls and 350 letters a week, a check by British Telecom revealed that only about 12% of all calls made had succeeded in getting through' (EDA 2000).

Consequently in 1993, the EDA set up a project to establish service specifications for the treatment of anorexia and bulimia – this resulted in the publishing of a detailed report.
This report was aimed to 'improve the quality of care and its availability to all people with eating disorders' this was by:
1. 'Providing recommendations to purchasers on appropriate services for people with eating disorders.
2. Promoting examples of good practise.
3. Encouraging training in eating disorders for all professionals.'(EDA 2000)

Although compiled mainly for the benefit and use of people involved professionally with the treatment of eating disorders, it also contains information of great value to all those involved with eating disorders. The report will be quoted from throughout this chapter as an excellent source of reference, recommended by professionals as the most comprehensive report regarding the provision needed for the treatment of eating disorders; *'With regards to what is needed to provide a successful treatment service, I honestly don't think you can better the report published by the EDA'* (Chris Prestwood – see chapter 5).

The first thing that must be considered when providing/seeking treatment is ensuring that the service holds the right understanding of eating disorders and consequently the right ethos regarding treatment. As the EDA clearly states 'Eating disorders are not primarily about food; starving or binge eating are symptoms of underlying emotional and psychological disorders' any treatment service needs to acknowledge the essential point that to treat an eating disorder, the whole individual must be treated – not just the physical symptoms. In so many ways it seems extraordinary that there is still a lack of understanding and conclusive course of treatment.

Many media reports lead us to believe that eating disorders are a recent condition when in actual fact anorexia was first named in the last century and bulimia in the 1970's (EDA 2000). It would seem that there should, by now, be clear consensus, especially as most eating disorders occur between the ages of 15 and 25 years (anorexia has appeared in children as young as 8 but bulimia is rare before the age of 13), if not understood and treated properly then people stand to lose some of the most valuable years of their lives.

Indeed, if not treated promptly and correctly, eating disorders can become so deeply entrenched that they are extremely difficult to treat and can often become chronic 'the sooner the eating disorder is recognised and given help the better the prognosis' (EDA 2000).

In the first instance, there are several diagnostic criteria, which practitioners should check for when presented with a patient who is either showing certain physical problems (which do not have another explanation) or have been escorted by an anxious relative/friend.

For Anorexia these include; 'refusal to maintain a body weight for age and height (i.e. weight loss of 15% below that expected or failure to make expected weight gain during a period of growth), In females, absence of at least three consecutive menstrual cycles, increasing isolation from friends, perfectionism and other obsessions, ritualistic behaviour' etc (EDA 2000).

When Bulimia is suspected amongst the most common indicators are; 'recurrent episodes of binge eating, recurrent inappropriate compensatory behaviour in order to prevent weight gain e.g. use of laxatives, diuretics, feeling out of control, helpless and lonely, secretive behaviour' etc (EDA 2000).

In the light of such indicators, practitioners need to consider the possibility of an eating disorder as being a likely diagnosis.

Although many reports into the success rates of treatments for eating disorders are often over pessimistic, being based on severely ill patients who have tried treatments before, it could well be that better provision of the right treatment could improve more general statistics.

Recent studies have shown that for anorexia: 50% of sufferers reach life in recovery, 30% retain partial behaviours and 20 % live with the chronic condition, in a follow up study, 76% were successfully living in recovery (EDA 2000). For bulimia: half of sufferers become free of bulimic symptoms and attitudes after treatment, a follow up study of 50 patients showed that 52% had fully recovered, 30% had a mild residual disorder, 9% had a partial eating disorder and 9% had the full disorder. A small number of sufferers do die, particularly where there are associated problems with drugs, alcohol or self-mutilation (EDA 2000).

It would be interesting to know how many of those in recovery after many years and those who were not in recovery could have been helped more through prompt/better treatment. This is particularly of concern as Anorexia has the highest death rate of all psychiatric illness, this being as a result of suicide, starvation or heart failure.

However, whilst it is easy to say that prompt diagnosis and correct treatment are of great importance, there are many problems faced by professionals in making a diagnosis. Although recognition and diagnosis are essential, as a person cannot gain access to services without it, there is often trouble with recognising the early signs. Patients will often try to disguise the condition, will be reluctant to admit to having a problem (may be ashamed to), may not be forthcoming about important symptoms, this could well be because they have grave fear of the consequences and a possible perceived lack of confidentiality.

If, as mentioned previously, the professional in question does not have relevant training/understanding they will not be able to see past the deception for the more subtle signs or will not know the right questions to ask/way to ask them. When the condition is not recognised, the patient may be sent to inappropriate services, a patient may be sent to a physician for infertility or gastro-intestinal problems (for example). Conversely however there are occasionally medical conditions, which are misdiagnosed as being an eating disorder. This may be due to the increased media interest in the condition and consequently GP's and other professionals are anxious not to miss diagnosing an eating disorder.

Often, once a person has been accurately diagnosed with an eating disorder they may then be referred to the practise counsellor (or possibly a private counsellor). This, of course, can be very effective as one of the most important aspects of reaching recovery from an eating disorder is to talk through the issues that are causing difficulties. However, counselling can only be effective if, the counsellor has knowledge of anorexia/bulimia, is available and has access to specialist advice when necessary.

It is also important that counsellors have professional supervision as problems can arise if there is not medical professional taking responsibility for monitoring the status and progress of the individual physically.

Local mental health services can be helpful for some people with eating disorders but often they are poorly equipped to really be of benefit to many sufferers. The skills and expertise in treating eating disorders amongst professionals working in local mental health services vary enormously. The involvement in such a service is often the result of the persons own interest and initiative rather than part of a planned approach to treatment, unfortunately even once they have acquired the necessary expertise they will often encounter problems in allocating necessary time for patients. It is often also the case that staff working in a local service will lack experienced professional supervision and access to specialist information, which is required to maintain their own personal resources.

Many patients with eating disorders need long-term intensive therapy, with the continuity of a therapist with whom they can build trust and confidence, owing to the rather precarious structure of many local services (often linked to funding difficulties) such continuity of care if not always available. Perhaps rather disturbingly an area lacking in assessment is the effectiveness of primary and local mental health services, and many sufferers of eating disorders have actually found experiences with such services as very detrimental.

When being treated within a local service, if an eating disorder reaches the severity that is considered to be life threatening, the person will often be admitted to a general adult psychiatric in-patient unit. In such a situation the treatment is often aimed only at weight gain without addressing underlying psychological issues, this is without doubt extremely damaging to the long-term prognosis for the patient. Any treatment within a general psychiatric unit is likely to be ineffective if, as is often the case, the staff do not have specific knowledge about eating disorders. It is also true to say that the death rates amongst people with anorexia 'over 20 years is much lower for those treated in specialist centres rather than in a general psychiatric unit' (EDA 2000).

With regards to children and adolescents, a 'recent study found that few GP's and only a third of paediatricians thought of eating disorders as a possible diagnosis when presented with case studies of children with weight loss and who were not eating' (EDA 2000). Children are most likely to be referred to general paediatric clinics, unfortunately this, as with most referrals within the NHS, may mean assessment and appropriate treatment is delayed. Also the staff within general clinics (as with general staff within adult psychiatric units) are unlikely to have any experience of eating disorders.

It is the case that the majority of specialist programmes are developed in adult mental health services and there are few services specifically designed for children and adolescents. This is rather a ridiculous situation, as it appears to be in spite of the fact that the illness usually begins during adolescence. Unless living in the area of one of the few services specifically for children they may receive little actual treatment, this is most serious as they become severely emaciated much more rapidly than older sufferers and muscle tissue breaks down at a much earlier stage in the disorder. Obviously this is extremely dangerous as recovery, (if it is reached) will be riddled with serious physical consequences, which will be of long duration.

Adolescents are often treated either with much younger children, which can be most embarrassing, or with adults, which can be equally uncomfortable. As someone who suffered through my teenage years I know how deeply destructive to the rest of life it can be, and yet I was lucky in that I managed to complete my education. Many who develop the illness during childhood or adolescence may miss out on much, if not all, of the most valuable years of their education. In a society that places so much weight on the worth of, and necessity for, quality education, it can greatly hamper recovery if the patient cannot see a future for themselves. It is therefore essential for such patients to receive encouragement, support and advice to enable them to see that it is possible for them to build a real life for themselves. This is of course another aspect of the illness, which is unlikely to be provided by a local service with limited funds and specialist staff.

The importance of patients being referred to a specialist service cannot be emphasised enough, I spent over a year falling deeper into the grip of the illness whilst receiving 'treatment' from a local service and I have met many other sufferers who have experienced a similar situation. 'The average age of presentation of a patient at a specialist service is 20-25 years, after the individual has had a disorder for an average of 5 years' (EDA 2000) by this point the prognosis is often very poor as the illness and consequent thoughts feelings and actions can be deeply entrenched. Also the physical condition is often very serious due to the prolonged malnutrition/damage from other illness-induced behaviours.

As desperate as the need for specialist services is, there are many areas of the U.K where there are not any in existence; most centres of excellence are in London and South East. These specialist centres simply can not meet the demand for services, 'in 1992 a survey by the Royal College of Psychiatrists found that only about 1500 new patients a year were seen. This was just over two thirds of the referrals received, only about 25% of patients seen came from outside the catchment area' (EDA 2000).

The number of people in desperate need of help who are simply not able to receive it is extremely worrying, they are either not being accurately diagnosed and referred for proper treatment, they live in the wrong area or the waiting lists are such that they are simply waiting.

The question is unfortunately often not when they will receive treatment but if they will survive with the illness long enough for their name to come to the top of the list.

The predictors for poor prognosis as set out in the EDA report should be considered when any service is attempting to treat a sufferer, these being; age of onset, duration, disturbed family relations, previous psychotherapy and low weight. This is not to say that sufferers fulfilling any or all of these criteria should be deemed as beyond help, but more that those within the service should be aware that the treatment is likely to need to be of long duration. It is however, most positive to state that studies have shown that reaching recovery is possible even if the patient has lived for years in the depths of an eating disorder, be it Anorexia or Bulimia. It is also considered that 'patient mortality increases with the length of follow up treatment' (EDA 2000) this is to say, any treatment service which does not provide any follow up treatment is not really fulfilling the needs of it's patients as relapse or even more serious consequence is likely without such attention.

There are of course, serious medical implications associated with suffering from either anorexia or bulimia. With regards to anorexia, the full effects of starvation include the following – gastric problems, poor circulation, electrolyte imbalance, heart failure, infertility, kidney failure, osteoporosis and possible epilepsy. The long-term consequences of anorexia can include stunted growth and severe osteoporosis.

Bulimia can cause gastro-intestinal problems including stomach cramps and constipation. Also, vomiting, diuretic and laxative abuse can cause fluid and electrolyte disturbance although, such complaints are likely to disappear as the patient recovers. However, the long term consequences can include throat ulcers and tooth erosion from the action of stomach acids, these may also damage the oesophageal sphincter muscles and laxative abuse can cause bowel damage.

Such medical consequences give yet further credibility to the belief that eating disorders must be treated as promptly as possible. In order to make any treatment worthwhile to all those involved, it must be considered and understood exactly what is most likely to produce the most effective treatment and the best possible positive outcome.

The EDA finds, (strongly supported by Chris Prestwood – chapter 5) and many patients would agree, that it is a real eclectic approach to treatment that is most likely to benefit patients and there are certain specific areas that need to be included. For example it is very important to consider that the triggers leading to the manifestation of the illness are often multiple and each individual will have a combination of contributory factors – these could be personal, familial, social and cultural. It is also essential to accept that what is appropriate to one patient may not be appropriate to another, the individual must be taken into account at all times.

Aspects of treatment that can be of benefit within an eclectic approach are most varied, and it is providing a wide range of group and individual therapies that can make all the difference to the success (or not) of treatment. This approach clearly takes into account that each patient is an individual and will benefit from different things (as mentioned above). The type of approaches included within such a service could be any combination (or ideally all) of the following; counselling and psychotherapy are virtually invaluable in the treatment of eating disorders as they 'aim to address the underlying emotional and psychological issues' (EDA 2000); this is as opposed to the focus on weight gain so often concentrated on within treatment programmes.

Cognitive Behaviour Therapy concentrates on the specific beliefs that the individual holds which underlie their behaviour. The aim is to challenge their beliefs and consequently alter their behaviour.

Life Skills focuses on the sorts of behaviours and emotions that need to be controlled/changed/modified/acquired in order to assist people to return to, and cope within, normal life after treatment.

Anxiety management, anger management, relaxation techniques, communication skills and assertiveness training can all prove most helpful.

Creative Therapies such as psychodrama, art, drama and music therapy can help people recognise and express painful feelings that may be blocked by the eating disorder.

Family Therapy and Family Counselling involves assessing how family members communicate and manage conflict, exploring how this might affect the person with the disorder.

Nutritional Counselling is essential for all patients with eating disorders, many sufferers will not have eaten 'normally' for a very long time – if ever, therefore without carefully structured advice their eating will suffer outside of hospital even if they are determined that it will not.

Exercise Groups are often essential if excessive exercise has been identified as being one of a patient's associated behaviours. Such a group will help patients to understand what an appropriate and safe amount of exercise is and will hopefully lead to enjoyment of exercise in a healthy way.

Drug Therapy can be very useful in helping sufferers reach a position when they can begin to work through some of the deeper issues. Anti depressants are often prescribed to help with the depression that so regularly accompanies eating disorders. They can also be used specifically for Bulimia to reduce bingeing and purging (although they are not usually effective in the long term). These should only ever be used in conjunction with other therapies however and only then if deemed absolutely necessary.

Treatment services will not necessarily be able to offer all the above types of approach and often centres will be selective with regards to which patients are offered/required to attend certain groups. For example, an exercise group may be reserved for those patients in whom an exercise behaviour has been identified, therefore needs must be carefully assessed in order for a persons time in treatment to be as beneficial as possible.

It would appear that certain approaches within treatment can be more beneficial to a specific eating disorder and others are thought to be useful for all sufferers. For example, for sufferers of anorexia, family therapy seems to be essential for children under 16 and young adolescents and very beneficial for adolescents still living at home and is considered to be helpful to adults also. It is interesting to note that family therapy can take different forms than the name would suggest, whereby the family and the individual can actually meet with the therapist at different times – this can help with any inhibitions anyone may have speaking in front of their family and can also reduce the intensity of the, almost inevitable, feelings of guilt.

Cognitive behavioural therapy is seen to be of particular worth for sufferers of Bulimia in reducing target behaviours and improving general mental health. They are also seen to benefit considerably from intensive individual therapy and 'self help' manuals can be useful alongside existing treatments and can reduce the amount of time spent with the psychotherapist. The EDA operates a ten week telephone programme for women with bulimia, wherever they live and under the medical supervision of their GP.

This programme includes keeping a diary to record food and feelings, a weekly appointment with their GP and a weekly counselling session over the phone with the EDA. The programme also operates a series of follow up phone calls every three months for two years and the whole process has proved helpful for many sufferers.

Unfortunately, 'out of 21 specialist centres identified as "specialist" 10 has a nurse with specialist knowledge, 12 had a dietician, 14 offered a session with a psychologist – less than half had a specialist social worker, occupational therapist or physiotherapist' (EDA 2000). In spite of the clear benefits of an eclectic approach, even services defined as specialist are still not able to provide all that may be considered helpful in the treatment of eating disorders.

A further consideration is that outcome measures are often not easily defined, the results of professional studies do not always agree with how individuals view their own recovery. For the treatment of anorexia, weight gain and menstruation are often used as benchmarks in research studies, purely physical signs are not good measures however as for some sufferers it may be an acceptable outcome that they maintain a weight that is still below normal but they can cope with and it is enough for them to function. Also, becoming a normal weight does not, on its own, represent being in recovery. Indeed, for the majority of people with anorexia, the hardest work begins once a target weight is reached (i.e. the sufferer no longer has the illness to mask feelings). To view the gaining of weight as criteria for measuring recovery is really far too simplistic.

Also for those suffering from Bulimia, a normal body weight is often maintained throughout the period of their illness and to use weight, as a guide in these cases is totally inaccurate in the first instance, let alone as a measure of successfully reaching recovery.

There are certain aspects of providing a successful treatment service that have been identified within the EDA report, these recommendations are aimed at assisting health authorities to provide services that are both successful and affordable but are also most helpful to those seeking treatment or investigating the possibilities for someone close to them.

These recommendations include early recognition of the illness; training for all those involved with young people to assist in recognising the signs and individual, group and family treatments available locally.

The report also highlights the types of treatment that are ineffective and indeed can be deeply detrimental, for example – 'Behaviour modification' involves linking weight gain or 'good' eating habits with rewards. The patient may start with strict bed rest in a bare room with gradual rewards, 'studies have not found any long-term benefit from strict behavioural regimes. Patients see it as abusive and coercive which further reduces their self-esteem' (EDA 2000).

Appetite stimulants used to be prescribed for people with anorexia but are no longer considered appropriate 'they have not lost their appetite but the ability to let themselves eat' (EDA 2000).

In some ways such treatment seems tame in comparison to the barbaric practise of electro convulsive therapy (ECT), which proposes to 'cure' the individual by sending an electric current through the brain. The positive results of such treatment are non-existent and the negative physical and, indeed psychological, consequences can last forever. Many people I was in treatment with had received several courses of ECT prior to their admission to the programme. I was absolutely horrified as I had held the naïve view that such things had disappeared into the vault of disgraceful medical practises along with blood letting and the like. Indeed, only last year there was the dreadfully shocking case of a celebrity who died after receiving an operation to the brain, which was believed would restore her appetite and 'cure' her anorexia.

Such dire lack of understanding of the illness leading to a dangerous, ultimately fatal, operation should clearly not be happening in this advanced medical age. Through reading the personal accounts (see chapter 3) it can be seen that people often receive treatment that is extremely damaging and they waste a great deal of precious time being subjected to detrimental, often humiliating experiences.

Effective treatment should help the individual to take control of their life, including their eating, it cannot be forced upon them as the instant they leave treatment they will be vulnerable to the illness once more. True recovery can only be obtained through treatment that deals with the underlying emotional and psychological aspects that have fuelled the eating disorder. Similarly the treatment service must also assist the person in learning to live and function in the real world (i.e. the world outside of a treatment unit), without the illness that has dominated their thoughts, feelings and actions for so long – possibly all their lives.

Whether the service is a private centre or an NHS one, the principals of practise need to be the same if they are to truly benefit the patient. The situation identified by the EDA that 'few health authorities identify eating disorders as part of their mental health strategy', needs to change in order of people to receive the treatment they need.

There is no doubt that eating disorders can be successfully treated but the service must treat the whole of the illness and therefore the whole of the person if true life in recovery is to be achieved.

People with eating disorders suffer to such a deep and cruel extent throughout their time with the illness, the very least they deserve is to receive real treatment through a service with the correct ethos and the appropriate provision of care.

Chapter 7.   Little Steps.

The real key to fighting the illness is the belief in a life in recovery. A real life. No words can truly describe the horror of existing with the illness, every day so dark, the feelings so desperate that it is beyond any description.

Working towards recovery can a dark terrifying place too, but there is a point when the days begin to grow brighter and, almost without warning, there is a future to be grasped with both hands. The work then must go into keeping that future.

My 'key worker' whilst in hospital said something to me that I often remind myself of 'you cannot change the past that has happened, you can only change the past that is to come', the illness caused me to dwell on the past and all the things that had happened for which I could blame myself. This (coupled with more recent events) gave the illness all the fuel it needed. People in the grip of an eating disorder must be helped to deal with the past and the issues it imposed if they are to move forward.

Anyone involved with eating disorders needs to understand just how damaging the negative thought processes can be and in spite of the best intentions of the individual, they can be overwhelmingly powerful. Those close to someone with an eating disorder need to hold on to the person they know, not the person the illness causes them to appear. The experience of an eating disorder is incredibly hard for relatives and friends, but I hope that through the contents of this book, they will see that they are not alone in their thoughts and feelings.

The most important thing to remember is that no one is to blame, eating disorders are an illness and whatever the root cause may be, they are no different to any other illness, they just happen. Indiscriminately. Whilst the triggers that cause the manifestation of it may be partly accountable to specific events, the responsibility of blame for the illness is not anyone's to take. Whether or not one feels responsible for being 'a trigger' it is essential not to focus on this but to work with the sufferer to resolve the situation and move forward. The feeling of helplessness is very understandable as so often sufferers seem beyond reach and treatment seems impossible to obtain, what is important is to explore all avenues, push for attention from professionals and (most importantly) offer love and support. I know that no one could ask for more.

Obtaining treatment may seem difficult but it is out there and if no joy is given through one GP/consultant then go to another! The prompt admission to a service offering the right treatment with specialist staff and an eclectic approach is absolutely essential for life in recovery to be achieved.

No one in the world would choose to 'live' with an eating disorder and they need and deserve all the help, love and support necessary to help them through. With my incomparable family, husband and dogs, in addition to my ambitions and dreams I have so much to keep fighting for and I am determined to do just that.

No matter how hard it may be, I firmly believe that life in recovery can be achieved. I am living it, and every day that anorexia does not control is a day for which I am so grateful.

Every little step taken is one closer to a real life and a real future.

References

Eating Disorders Association - A Guide to Purchasing and Providing Services 2000 (Report 1993)

Margo 1987; Schneider and Agras 1987 - Study into Men with Eating Disorders.

Van Elburg et al 1994 – Study into Genetic basis for Eating Disorders

Adan et al 2001 – Study into AgRP link to Anorexia.

Lask et al, Study into biological brain activity. 2005

.
Peggy Claude Pierre - The Secret Language of Eating Disorders.
Doubleday (division of) Transworld Publishers Ltd 1998

For information and advice on all aspects of eating disorders:

Eating Disorders Association
First Floor
Wensum House
103 Prince of Wales Road
Norwich
NR1 1DW

Helpline – (01603) 621 414

Youth line – (01603) 765 050

Recorded Message – (0906) 302 0012

Printed in the United Kingdom
by Lightning Source UK Ltd.
106715UKS00001B/16-63